The Catholic Girl's Guide to Sex

The Catholic Girl's Guide to Sex

Melinda Anderson and Kathleen Murray

illustrated by Alli Arnold

BROADWAY BOOKS
New York

We dedicate this book to

Loretta Anderson

and Joan Murray,

who have always guided our more serious

moral compasses and whom we love and admire.

PRINTED IN THE UNITED STATES OF AMERICA

BROADWAY BOOKS and its logo, a letter B bisected on the diagonal, are trademarks of Broadway Books, a division of Random House, Inc.

Visit our website at www.broadwaybooks.com

First edition published 2003

Library of Congress Cataloging-in-Publication Data
Anderson, Melinda, 1974–
The Catholic girl's guide to sex / Melinda Anderson and Kathleen Murray.—1st ed.
p.   cm.
Includes bibliographical references.
1. Catholic women—Sexual behavior. 2. Sex—Religious aspects—Catholic Church. 3. Sex—Humor.
I. Murray, Kathleen, 1977– II. Title.
HQ29.A53 2003
306.7'082—dc21
2003051803

ISBN 0-7679-1303-5

1 3 5 7 9 10 8 6 4 2

Authors' Note

The writing of *The Catholic Girl's Guide to Sex* began with an idea born more than two years ago. The journey from then until now was exhausting and exhilarating. We would like to thank those who helped us along the way.

First, to Jack Scovil, whose belief in this book gave us the confidence to write it. And whose good humor and practical advice made all the difference for these first-time authors. We are grateful to all the folks at Broadway Books and especially to our editor, Kris Puopolo, who shared our enthusiasm and sense of humor from the beginning. To Alli Arnold, whose excitement carried the final stages of this project and whose creativity blew our minds.

A special debt of appreciation goes to Marty Timins and to all the people who read this book while we wrote it: Eric Anderson, Brad Barnes, Kelsey Collins, Casey Harris (Jimmy McCracken), Caroline Heller and Whitney Lee. And a big thank you to Walter Anderson, whose edits, encouragement and advice guided us in more ways than we can mention.

We're especially grateful to Susan Abramson, Xanthe Alban-Davies, Claudia Anderson, Kathleen Bailey, Peter Bailey, Brian Barnes (Vincent Kelly), Todd Barnes (Danny Gallo), Jeff Beil, Vanessa Biery, Michael Counts, Wendy Dineen, Clay Enos, Lizzie Felleman, Marjie Fingeret, Lisa Giangrande, Tracey Gritz (Francesca Gallo), Francesco Grosso, Danielle Hall (Andrea Perez), Will Holden, Heather Kalish, Denise Koltis, Ted Koltis, Tom Koltis, Jenn Lee, Allison Luyten, Carlynn Magliano, Jenny Magliari (Iris Sullivan), Deborah Marinoff, Lauren Mayne, Casey Oetgen, Alexandra Penney, Caron Pinkus, Erin Pruitt, Gregory Pruitt, Josh Radin, Mary Robbins, Peter Rosenstreich, Josh Rubach, Emily Selcer, Lindsay Senter, Valerie Stivers, Tony Tedesco, Michelle Stern, Meredith Ullman, Dana Weissman, Sharon Wolfson. And Paul Tedesco, whose assistance was invaluable.

Finally, to our families, who have accepted the book with laughter and love. Thank you, thank you, thank you.

"Sex is something I really don't understand too hot . . . I keep making up these sex rules for myself, and then I break them right away."

—J. D. Salinger, *The Catcher in the Rye*

Contents

Dear Reader

Welcome, fellow Catholics and those of you who seek to better understand the inner workings of this mysterious bunch. You have arrived here, we imagine, for a variety of reasons. Some of you are like us—modern Catholic girls trying to reconcile our sexual relationships with him and our devotional relationship to *Him*. Or maybe you're on your way to becoming one of us: You're a teenage Catholic girl wandering aimlessly along a path fraught with confusion. You want answers. Others of you may be moms, like our own, looking to unlock the secrets of their daughters and the promiscuous world in which they were raised. And still more of you, we suspect, are men and women of all faiths, hoping to learn the scoop on the girls who seem sexiest at their most pious. We understand.

We spoke with dozens of guys and gals to get the goods. In certain cases we have purposely obscured the identities of our subjects at their request. We have done so faithfully to protect the innocent (and the guilty). In addition to their stories, you'll find lists, quizzes and tips throughout the book. Feel free to dip in and out of the pages to get your juices flowing.

We hope you enjoy reading this book as much as we enjoyed writing it. Now, let's get it on.

Chapter One

The Church

A little background:
Parochial education remembered

"When authorities warn you of the sinfulness of sex,
there is an important lesson to be learned:
Do not have sex with the authorities."

— MATT GROENING

You probably have a grasp of the Roman Catholic Church's beliefs, and some of you may know them well. However fruitful your tree of knowledge, we're going to give you a little Vatican 101. Maybe now you'll get why Catholics and sex are like oil and water. In this chapter, you'll learn the Church's stance on issues like birth control, sex education and homosexuality without complicated religious jargon. Think of it as Sunday school the way you want to hear it.

We pored over religious texts so that you don't have to. We recognize that we are not priests, nuns or Church historians, but we've been students all of our lives. While many in the Catholic Church can debate proper inference, the views expressed here are as we understand them. Remember, the Church argued for centuries about how many angels could dance on the head of a pin. We don't expect wholesale agreement. It's easy to see how so many modern Catholic girls get hung up.

Sin Today, Gone Tomorrow

The changing nature of Church law

Here's the deal: There are two types of law that govern all Catholics—divine law and Church law. Divine law is inherent; basically it's the rules of the Bible. On the other hand, the hierarchy of priests, bishops and, ultimately, the Pope formulates Church law. So, while divine law is fixed, Church law adapts and evolves whenever the Pope decides to change it. Once stated, it is fixed only until the next major change. What does this mean for you? A sin has a shelf life.

Anyone who lived through Vatican II (1962 to 1965), which provoked seminal change for the modern Catholic Church, will be well aware of how this works. Imagine your mother for a moment. Growing up, she probably heard Masses in Latin, endured tuna casserole every Friday and faced nuns who smacked. During high school, the rules changed: She listened to Masses in English, ate fish on Fridays during Lent only and met nuns who broke out the rulers strictly for math class. What constituted a sin her sophomore year didn't by the time she graduated. A similar feat may be true for you: What you repent today, your daughters may revel in tomorrow.

So you see, the Church does go with the flow, even if it sometimes seems like the Vatican calendar is set about 150 years behind the times.

You're probably like most Catholics who navigate between these two sets of standards—divine law and Church law—and evaluate your own moral conscience based upon some combination of the two. You may accept "thou shall not kill" but turn a blind eye to birth control, figuring Church law will catch up with reality some day. Here's the catch: As a Roman Catholic, it's a requirement to accept the infallibility of the Pope. This is *huge*. It's the major belief that separates us from other Christians. Methodists and Baptists and Greek Orthodox don't acknowledge the Pope as the supreme Christian leader. We do. In short, follow Church law or follow a different religion (and risk eternal damnation). Look, we're longing for loopholes, too, but we have to tell it like it is.

Now to the good (or not-so-good) stuff. Here's the 411 on Church and sex.

Bible Pop Quiz

In what form does God appear to Moses in Exodus 3:2?
  a.   Burning bush
  b.   Milking breast
  c.   Belly dancing harlot
  d.   Prancing drag queen

Answer: a

"Let priests and bishops denounce—let the hierarchy roar! They cannot push the chick back into the shell."

—Margaret Sanger

Catholic Curriculum

A little learnin' will do ya

Guess what? The Church is in favor of proper sex education. That's right. You heard it here. The Vatican actually lays out guidelines for it in 1983's *Educational Guidance in Human Love: Outlines in Sex Education.* In essence, the text spells out the fundamental meaning and values of human sexuality and the right use of sex based on one's stage in life. Right use of sex? Accept this: It pretty much boils down to limited use or no use at all. Thanks so much, your Holiness.

Premarital Prohibition

Single, celibate and chaste

Here's the simple truth: For any sexual act to pass muster, it must be committed between husband and wife *and* allow the possibility of procreation. Anything less (or more, as the case may be) leads the faithful away from God. Therefore, anyone not married is instructed to remain celibate. The intention to marry—as in actual two-carat ring, fuchsia bridesmaid dresses and at least a dozen fights with mom—does *not* count, even if the nuptials are planned for your local church.

Sexual sins can take two forms: one against chastity and the other against virtue. The first is obvious—fornication. The second, however, includes pornography and masturbation. That's right, self-love is out. If you're not getting randy to make a baby, you ain't supposed to do it. At all. So, in theory, it's the chaste life for us single gals.

Good Habits Die Hard

Some single folks take their commitment to remaining in God's good graces so seriously that they make a vow to remain chaste for life. They are called priests and nuns. They give it up only for God. Celibately speaking, there really is only one thing that separates you from them: You get to do it eventually. After the wedding. Other than that, the call to chastity is the same for us all.

The Gay Way

You may think the Church is a hothouse breeding homophobia, but that's not its intent. There has, in truth, been much advancement in its position regarding homosexuals. In fact, single gays and lesbians are meant to be treated the same way as single heteros. Strict, yes, but not sexual-orientation–biased, per se.

Basically, the Catholic Church's current view is love the sinner but hate the sin. Being a homosexual is not a sin—no more than being a heterosexual single person with desires is—but acting on those fantasies is sinful. Why? All acts of homosexuality are considered sins against chastity because—you got it—they go against natural law. There's no baby-making, so homo sex is no-no sex.

WordPlay

Agnostic

1. Someone who doubts the existence of God.

2. A potential husband; agnostics are more easily molded than more faithful subjects.

"I have spent a lot of time searching through the Bible for loopholes."

—W. C. Fields

The Bible Said What?!

Genesis 19, the tale of Sodom and Gomorrah, is often cited in Church discussions of homosexuality. The story is that God destroys those cities to punish the men who live there for their unnatural acts. (Get it? Sodomy.)

Anyway, angels go to Lot's house to stay with the good man for the night. Evil townsmen come to the house and demand to have intimacies with the angels. Lot refuses to let them in, but—get this—he offers up his virgin daughters to the men to do with as they please. Hmmmm??? Read it for yourself.

And oh, but wait, there's more! Lot's daughters eventually get their own father drunk and "lie with him," ultimately bearing two children by him. Who needs Stephen King horror stories when you have the Good Book on your bedside table?

Wedded Bliss and Birth (un)Controlled

What it means for the marrieds

So how is it that so many Catholic families have gaggles of kids? That's easy. Prior to Vatican II, the Church's position was simple: The purpose of sexual intercourse was solely procreation (read: no birth control whatsoever). Vatican II changed that, if only slightly, by acknowledging that married couples have a right to limit the size of their family. Further, the Church recognized "mutual self-giving" (does that sound racy or what?) as another major plus of sexual intercourse and one that is good for committed married couples. So how can a husband and wife plan to mutually self-

WordPlay

Atheist

1. Someone who denies the existence of God.

2. Your boyfriend, whose existence you might deny to your mom; she doesn't believe atheists actually exist.

give and still have a small family? Welcome to the rhythm nation—the only acceptable method of birth control.

As for what's on the pleasure menu, our married brethren are not so different from us singles. Before you rush to get married and see your sin factor drop, ask yourself this: "Can I get pregnant from acts other than straight-up sex?" Unless you find a way to carry your eggs in your esophagus, oral sex is out. You get the point here, yes? Even married life excludes nonprocreative acts.

You may have your own moral beliefs about what a married couple should or shouldn't be allowed to do (or use while doing so) behind closed doors. Rest assured, you're not alone. And it's not just us lay people. Scores of bishops, pastors and theologians have questioned the Church's seemingly antiquated doctrine. As yet it remains unchanged.

Note: Lots of gay couples want the Church to recognize same-sex marriages. In that way, they hope, the sex acceptability factor will shoot straight up. Thus far, these requests have been met with a big fat "no."

Severed Ties

Divorced and doing it

A Catholic woman was once married but then called it quits. Does this exempt her in any way from returning to the chaste life? She's done it already, right? Guess again, sister. Not only is she sinning against her chastity, but she is also breaking the sixth commandment. And we're thinking adultery is seriously frowned upon at the pearly gates.

How is this possible, you ask? It's all right there in

Matthew 19:9, which basically says that anyone who divorces and marries another is committing adultery unless the marriage is unlawful (read: qualifies for an annulment). Pretty heavy stuff.

Life Sentence

Guilt with no escape

You may have been born post–Vatican II, in calmer, gentler times. But the folks who raised you—your parents, teachers and clergy—were not. And though they tried to adapt their lessons to the evolving Church teachings, they were still stuck with guilt. Intentionally or not, they passed it along to you. Your cage of shame was sealed shut. Whether you choose to take or leave the doctrine, the Pope is still on your back. You're Catholic until you convert (and even then you'll probably still freak out a little).

> "To hear many religious people talk, one would think God created the torso, head, legs and arms but the devil slapped on the genitals."
>
> —Don Schrader

WordPlay

Jew

1. A member of the faith and culture of Judaism. Basically, Jews don't believe in the whole New Testament thing or Jesus being the Son of God.

2. Our heroes for maintaining a guilt-ridden existence regarding morality, work ethic and education but remaining largely guilt-free when it comes to sex.

3. What Jesus was. That's right, Jesus was no Catholic!

Are You Really Catholic or Just Conscious of Your Reputation?

After reading about the Church's sexual positions, you may think: "Of course I feel morally conflicted after engaging in not-so-sacred acts. But don't all girls, Catholic or otherwise?" Probably. There is a big difference between feeling the twangs of guilt and the wrath of God. You may just be worried that you'll be labeled loosey-goosey. We Catholics are worried about being marked for hell. Take this quiz to find out which "guilt group" you fall into.

1. You've had a terrific first date. The conversation flowed as easily as the wine. As a good girl, you should:

    a. Invite him in for a nightcap. He *did* pay, after all.

    b. Get a little for yourself. Rounding third seems appropriate for a first date.

    c. Say a sweet goodbye with a cordial kiss on the cheek. Remember, wherever two are gathered, Jesus is with you.

2. You lose your virginity. That's right, your big day has finally arrived. Now your biggest fear is:

    a. You're pregnant.

    b. That's as good as it gets.

    c. You will be struck down by lightning if you don't get to confession immediately.

3. When doing the walk of shame after a crazy night with your current love, you're feeling:

    a. A little embarrassed, because you're the only one in a miniskirt and tube top at ten on a Sunday morning.

    b. Slightly remorseful, because you just spent the night with your ex-boyfriend's best friend.

    c. A compelling need to march yourself right into the nearest church, bathe yourself with holy water, say ten rosaries and sit through Mass.

If you've answered mostly *as* or *bs*, get over it. You're not suffering from a truly guilty conscience; you're just concerned with looking respectable. Exception: You may be a lapsed Catholic. If so, beware. The Church might come back to haunt you. Lapses lapse, and the guilt could rebound big time.

If you've answered mostly *cs*, you're one of us: a true Catholic bound to feel ashamed—at least on some level, of every sexual inclination you've ever had—*forever*.

Don't Know Much About Biology

The angst over birth control is played out in a battle between us modern Catholic girls and the Church. For each scientific advancement in birth control (score one point for Us), there is a strict condemnation of contraception from the Vatican, leaving Catholic girls five steps behind (deduct five points). Check out how the score is settled:

US	THEM
1925 The first American-manufactured diaphragms are released.	**1930** Pope Pius XI's encyclical *Casti Connubii* (*On Christian Marriage*) proclaims the Vatican's opposition to marital birth control.
1951 Pope Pius XII addresses the Italian Catholic Society of Midwives and first gives explicit permission for use of the rhythm method in certain cases.	**1951** In same address, Pius XII continues to condemn artificial contraception.
1955 The first birth-control pill is developed by doctors Gregory Pincus and John Rock (a devout Catholic).	**1958** Pope Pius XII permits the use of the birth-control pill in limited medical situations. He doesn't count having ten kids among them.
1960 The FDA approves oral contraception.	

1964 IUD becomes broadly obtainable.

1988 The FDA approves the cervical cap.

1990 The introduction of Norplant in the U.S.

1992 Depo-Provera becomes available in the U.S.

1993 The female condom makes its debut.

2000 The birth-control patch is presented and testing is begun.

1968 Pope Paul VI ignores the Papal Birth Control Commission's vote to drop the ban on contraception and publishes the encyclical *Humanae Vitae*, officially prohibiting all use of artificial birth control.

1975 The Vatican issues the *Declaration on Certain Questions Concerning Sexual Ethics,* reaffirming the Church's condemnation of artificial birth control.

1981 Pope John Paul II's Apolistic Exhortation *Familiaris Consortio* maintains the ban on artificial contraception.

1993 On the twenty-fifth anniversary of *Humanae Vitae,* Pope John Paul II reiterates the Vatican's opposition to artificial contraception.

1994 *The Catechism of the Catholic Church* upholds the ban on artificial contraception.

For Us: 10 points	Against Us: 40 points

Final Tally

The year 2018 will mark the fiftieth anniversary of *Humanae Vitae.* Its tenets are sure to be revisited. And reiterated? Hopefully not. It just may be our chance to tilt the scales toward freedom. Well, not likely . . . but a girl can dream, can't she?

On the Other Hand

There are religious leaders who fanatically uphold Vatican law, and then there are noted Catholics who publicly oppose popular Church belief. The latter class of Catholics fights for birth-control rights and for the modern Catholic girl. Here are a few shining moments:

1961   John F. Kennedy, the first (and only) Catholic President, endorses reproductive research.

1963   Pope John XXIII establishes the Papal Birth Control Commission to reassess the Church's position.

1966   The Papal Birth Control Commission votes 52–4 to drop the ban on artificial birth control in marriage. (Unfortunately, Pope Paul VI ignores their vote.)

1968   More than six hundred Catholic theologians sign a statement in opposition to Paul VI's encyclical *Humanae Vitae,* which opposes artificial contraception.

1973   The National Fertility Survey reports that 68 percent of all U.S. Catholic women of reproductive age use a form of birth control that is prohibited in *Humanae Vitae.* In women aged 20 to 24, it's 78 percent.

1973   Catholics for a Free Choice is founded. (If you can believe it, this pro-choice organization is still going strong.)

1984   Ninety-seven Catholics, including twenty-six prominent religious figures, sign an ad in the *New York Times* asking for a renewed discussion on abortion.

1992   A Gallup poll reports that 81 percent of Catholic respondents said it was possible to be a good Catholic and publicly disagree with the Church's teaching.

WordPlay

WASP

1. White Anglo-Saxon Protestant.

2. A member of a Christian faith who broke ties with Rome.

3. Purveyors of mayonnaise, pearls and hyphenated last names.

"Well-behaved women rarely make history."
—Laurel Thatcher Ulrich

Lewd Ladies of the Bible

Let's face it. The Bible is among the steamiest works of literature ever written. From infidelity to incest, its stories have the makings of a juicy soap opera. Modern Catholic girls would play only a small walk-on role compared with the star power of these haughty heroines. Welcome to *The Days of Our Wives* starring:

Eve—The Original Bad Girl

Genesis 3

She takes a bite of the forbidden fruit, tempted by its power of infinite knowledge. She shares it with her man. They both become acutely aware of the sinful act, and their two curious souls eventually succumb to prohibited passion.

Tamar the Widow—The Manipulative Mother

Genesis 38

A childless widow, Tamar dresses in veils to seduce her father-in-law, Judah, in hopes of becoming pregnant. Months later, a palace guard brings the pregnant Tamar before Judah, who orders this woman to be burned to death for carrying illegitimate children. Tamar then reveals the paternity of her bastard child and gains amnesty from the befuddled Judah.

Potiphar's Wife—The Seductress Who Hankered for the Hired Help

Genesis 39

This nameless nymph yearns for her husband's handsome new servant, Joseph (not Jesus' stepdad). She relentlessly demands of

Joseph to lie with her, yet day after day he refuses. Enraged (and aroused) by his rejection, she frames the loyal minion and cries rape, thus sending the innocent soul to prison.

Delilah—The Gold Digger

Judges 16

Delilah agrees to seduce and destroy Samson for money. She uses his love against him as she schemes and manipulates to reveal the secret of his strength. He falls prey to her unscrupulous taunts and admits his one weakness—a secret that leads to his murder.

Jezebel—Lady of the Manor

1 Kings 21 and 2 Kings 9

She craves power and will stop at nothing to achieve it—sex, murder, whatever it takes. Using her painted eyes, Jezebel tries to get what she wants, ordering the death of any dissenter, even her own family members, to ensure her place on the throne. Her palace becomes a breeding ground for sexual immorality.

Bathsheba—The Beauty Queen

2 Samuel 11

While bathing under the summer sun, Bathsheba attracts the attention of King David. Her beauty mesmerizes him. He summons her. Even though she is a married woman, Bathsheba surrenders to his seductiveness. Upon discovering Bathsheba's pregnancy, David sends her husband to his death and takes her as his queen.

Herodias—The Scheming Bigamist

Mark 6

She commits bigamy by marrying her husband Philip's brother, Herod. John the Baptist—always the saintly one—disapproves of the relationship. Herodias schemes to use her own daughter in sexually compromising ways to get John's head on a silver platter.

Bible Pop Quiz

Match these bad girls of the Bible with their story:

1) The Woman at the Well

2) Lot's Wife

3) Sapphira

4) The Sinful Woman

5) The Lady from Endor

6) Athaliah

a. Stalker: followed Jesus to dinner, kissed his feet and poured perfume on them

b. Polygamist: had five husbands

c. Liar: succumbed to greed

d. Disbeliever: turned into pillar of salt

e. Mass-murderer: enough said

f. Psychic: practiced "witchcraft"

Answers: 1–b, 2–d, 3–c, 4–a, 5–f, 6–e

Roving Reporter

We sent our intrepid reporter to poll fellow Catholics on different sex issues. You'll find their responses throughout the book. Here we go: "How do the Church's views factor into your sex life?"

Vincent Kelly, 50
Married with ten kids

"We have a color-coded calendar above our bed. Any more questions?"

Jimmy McCracken, 15
Fordham Prep sophomore

"Not at all. I'm more of a fly-by-the-seat-of-my-pants, throw-caution-to-the-wind Catholic. You know, a rebel."

Danny and Francesca Gallo, both 29
Newlyweds

Francesca answers for both:
"We admit it. We use birth control. But we're in love, and we discussed it with our very cool priest. Anyway, our kids are definitely getting raised Catholic."
(In truth, Francesca only discusses birth control with her pharmacist, Jack Feelgood. But Danny does talk to a priest regularly when he goes to confession to receive absolution for the dirty, dirty deeds Francesca prefers.)

Iris Sullivan, 65
Unmarried

"I'm a 65-year-old unmarried virgin. How do you think they factor in? But if I knew then what I know now, I would have done it and done it some more."

Andrea Perez, 22
Recent college grad

"I take what I want and leave the rest behind."

"Sex is not a sin. Many people have complained that this is taking all the fun out of sex."

—Dr. Ruth Westheimer

In the Biblical Sense

Quite zestfully, the Good Book uses a vast catalog of catchwords to describe sexual acts. Check out the list below of our eleven favorite biblical euphemisms:

1. Give his wife her conjugal rights
2. To lie with
3. Let me come into you
4. Playing the harlot
5. Going after strange flesh
6. Cheer up his wife
7. Be fruitful and multiply
8. Went in unto
9. Pour out lust
10. Take our fill of love
11. To know

Song of Sex

For the steamiest passages in the Good Book, check out the Old Testament's Song of Songs. This biblical bit of erotica praises (and praises and praises) the mutual love of God and His people in decidedly mortal terms—the most pure of loves made human. And is it ever sexy. Try out some of the more descriptive lines on your paramour, and you're sure to get a rise out of him.

"Why should we take advice on sex from the Pope? If he knows anything, he shouldn't."

—George Bernard Shaw

Chapter Two

The Elders

Communication without excommunication:
The problem with sex education and
growing up Catholic

Catholic communication breakdown: Let's break it down.

Catholic girls don't talk sex (unless coerced by devilish authors). We've been speechless for years, mainly because we begin our lives with a definite communicative handicap—our parents. Sex talks in Catholic homes typically revolve around one of two catch phrases: "Open these [pointing to one's eyes] and close these [gesturing toward the young lass's legs]," or the simple and blunt "Sex, don't do it." And that's only if you're lucky enough to get a talk.

Health class is no help, either. Nuns answering questions about sex (even anonymous ones) do you no good. After years of biased information and misconstrued vocab (based primarily on playground banter), you enter your formative years ill-prepared for gossiping with the gals.

Read on to see how miraculous it is that you learned anything at all. But beware: Once you start talking, it isn't so easy to stop.

"All women become like their mothers. That is their tragedy. No man does. That is his."

—Oscar Wilde

Mom's the Word

Our first (but hopefully not last) source of sex ed

There are things in certain Catholic households that are never mentioned: sex, sex and—um, of course—sex. It is forbidden. No one is to speak, think, draw, listen, smell, see, dream, touch or entertain ideas about sex because it might just instigate the act. In these Catholic homes, the strong, silent type rules the roost. Other Catholic moms share the same no-sex-for-you mission as the my-lips-are-sealed mom, but they've adjusted their techniques. There's the random-sex-statement-spitting mom, the talk-about-sex-until-it's-not-sexy mom, the I'll-pretend-I'm-a-doctor mom . . . well, you get it. Read on for more on mom.

Silence Is a Virtue

Silent Catholic moms believe that talking about sex is like a gateway drug. If she does it a little, you'll do it a lot. So we don't ask, we don't tell, we don't know, they don't know. Good Catholic girls don't cross the line of ignorant bliss, because the reaction usually is lethal. Simple inquiries regarding the biological nature of reproduction are met with parental inquisitions: "Why do you need to know, you're

WordPlay

The birds and the bees

1. The facts about sex.

2. In a Catholic family, the birds and the bees are better left in the trees.

not having sex, ARE YOU!?" That is enough to shut us up for good.

Other Catholic moms can't even muster up enough moxie to sass back. They blush, shy away and flee the situation for a more pure chore like dusting, vacuuming or the laundry.

Another spin on the silent treatment is the sneak attack. It can take the form of a random remark while mom drops you off at a friend's house: "If you ever have sex, make sure the condoms don't have holes in them." Quickly exiting the car, you are half in shock at the mention of the word *condom* and half terrified by her rippage remark. Followed up days later with an artfully placed sex-can-stain-one's-reputation comment during a pizza party, mom shows that she knows when to hold 'em and when to throw 'em. She hopes that a well-timed remark punctuating her silence will be the key to chastity.

> "I wouldn't have turned out the way I was if I didn't have all those old-fashioned values to rebel against."
> —Madonna

Loud and Proud

Truly tricky moms (and dads) who cast aside the favored silent treatment use reverse psychology. We've seen this several times, and it's raw. It's when your mom finds a way to mention sex on any occasion, during any discussion: "Would you like French fries, onion rings or sex with your burger?" Or "Did you hear about the box of expired condoms that caused a girl to *ruin the rest of her life?*" Or at the table, she talks about the neighbor's cleaning lady's son: "He got his girlfriend pregnant. They both *ruined the rest of their lives.*"

It might start with your mother actually sitting you down to explain the technicalities of how babies are made. Don't be fooled that these moms are hip to the jive. These sex talks inevitably conclude with how you need to wait until marriage or else it will *ruin the rest of your life.* In these homes, the word *sex* isn't taboo, but that doesn't mean you are supposed to do it. Because, as you should know by now, sex can *ruin the rest of your life.*

Clinical-speak helps moms who want to avoid the sincere heart-to-heart but feel like they've imparted wisdom. They keep their words sterile as they yap it up for you. When certain biological situations arise, mom finds it appropriate to talk to you about sex. Case in point: menstruation.

On the first day of Ellen's period, for example, her mother explained how she was becoming a woman *mammary-glands/maxipads/menses* and how one becomes pregnant *sperm/ovum/zygote* after making love with the right man *penis/testes/scrotum.* Like a filibustering senator, this mom talks the talk endlessly but buries the issue beneath two tons of technical terms.

A variation is the loud-and-proud mom who believes she gave you all the right answers but doesn't realize (or even care) that her vagueness has kept you in the dark. Consider Denise: "I was allowed to ask my mom anything. But far from helping to decipher the truth, her answers confused me more. When I was seven, I asked her to define masturbation, something I understood to be very bad. She told me, 'It is playing with yourself.' Not realizing what kind of 'playing' she meant, I couldn't believe that every time I had Ken pick up Barbie in his red Corvette, I was masturbating."

"Where do babies come from? Don't bother asking adults. They lie like pigs."

—Matt Groening

A Prescription for Disaster

There *are* moms who recognize the need for a real talk. And for this they make an appointment with a gynecologist. Of course, they don't tell the doctor or the daughter that the point of the visit is not just to debrief but also to *debrief*. So a young girl gets her first Pap but no chat.

It might have been you who grasped the fact that your mother was zipped up. You tried to give mom a break and asked for Dr. Katz's phone number. All the girls at public school went to him, the hippest gyno in town. Rather than seize the opportunity to pass the buck, your Catholic mom flipped out because, in her view, seeing a private-parts physician signified sex. "Why," she thought, "would a virgin need a down-there doctor?" Diagnosis: perpetual ignorance.

Teach Our Children Well

Another Catholic parents' option for shifting responsibility is to bank on the Board of Education. Public-school tykes are in luck: You have a decent chance of learning something about sex in that special health class. Sure, the Church tries to get you to unlearn all that during CCD or CYO, but at least you have a fighting chance. Catholic-school kids, however, are more often kept in the dark. The lessons—if they exist at all— involve an archaic filmstrip from 1965 and are sandwiched between a Life of Jesus class and a morality exercise. Plus, every session includes a nod to the Church. What does this mean for you? You have to get the juice elsewhere.

We found two chalkboards used by health teachers. The first is credited to Sister Joanne. Ms. Shapiro, a public high school phys ed teacher, drew the second. The difference in artsistic rendering is rather astounding.

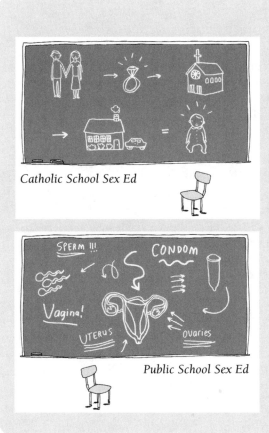

Catholic School Sex Ed

Public School Sex Ed

WordPlay

Catholic School

1. Parochial school devoted to educating young Catholics in the faith as well as about secular subjects.

2. If you didn't attend one, this is the place where other kids from your Church learned regular stuff and all about Jesus every day. Suckers.

CCD

1. Confraternity of Christian Doctrine, established to teach the faith to young Catholics who attend non-parochial schools.

2. If you didn't attend, this is the program where public-school kids who seemed cooler than the Catholic-school kids had to learn about Jesus outside of regular school (often on Sundays). Suckers.

Pre-K Pre-Cana

Erica was lucky enough to get a real sex talk. Even if it left her scarred for years.

"Despite their strict Catholic upbringing, my parents were very cool about talking sex with me. Back then, the only thing getting bigger by the day than my first-grade teacher Mrs. Collins's tummy were the rumors flying around as to why 'God put a baby in her!' 'She's very sick for a while and then a baby comes out in the toilet!' 'She's a whore!'

"So I finally asked my parents the question that makes every parent sweat, panic and often flee: 'Mommy, Daddy, where do babies come from?' They exchanged looks that made me know I had just embarked on a conversation for which they weren't prepared. Was I in trouble, I wondered? Could Chris O'Toole actually be right—that Mrs. Collins was bad to the bone? My mother, always the take-charge one, shooed my dad away and tried to explain S-E-X.

"She stressed, 'When two people fall in love, they go to Church and get married. Once they're married, they engage in a very special act called making love.' She went on to explain gently what making love consisted of, all the while stressing the following: love, marriage, church, fidelity, marriage, church.

"A few months later, I informed my parents that I would never be getting married. Confused, they asked, 'Erica, why don't you ever want to get married?'

"I responded, happy to set the record straight, 'If you think I'm gonna do what you said I had to do in front of Father Daly, you're out of your mind!'

"Although my mom was eager to clarify her lesson and explain that making love didn't actually happen *on the altar,* my dad hushed her up and let me go on believing it. He hoped I might never find out the truth and that his little girl would remain forever chaste."

Bible Pop Quiz

Which of the following is *not* a name for the devil?

a. Beelzebub
b. Lucifer
c. Sexually active single
d. Satan

Answer: c

Roving Reporter

Some Catholic parents like to sit down with their children and explain the birds and the bees. Most don't. "What did your mother teach you about sex?"

Vincent Kelly, 50
Married with ten kids

Blushing, "What? My mother? Sex? Oh Lord!"

Jimmy McCracken, 15
Fordham Prep sophomore

"I was like born knowing or something. It's a gift, really."

Danny and Francesca Gallo, both 29
Newlyweds

Francesca answers for both:
"It doesn't matter what his mom taught him. I taught him everything he knows. And how did I learn? My mom was really cool about talking sex. She was very open but always stressed values like waiting for the right man, getting him to love me first and saving myself. Thank God for mom. She really led by example."
(In truth, Francesca's mother doesn't even know the real paternity of her daughter and is frequently referred to around town as . . . well, let's just say she's known around town.)

Iris Sullivan, 65
Unmarried

"You mean Mother Superior? NOTHING. But if I had known she was a batty old nun, I would have done it and done it some more."

Andrea Perez, 22
Recent college grad

"If you're gonna use it, wrap it!"

"Sin, guilt, neurosis—they are one and the same, the fruit of the tree of knowledge."

—Henry Miller

Under Lock and Key: A Parental Guide to Your Skivvies

When shopping with your mom, you walk past Victoria's Secret. Do you stop? Well, if you answered "yes," you ain't Catholic, honey. Shopping sprees never include sexy bras and underwear—they are a predisposition to sex. They are for loose ladies. If it doesn't have a cotton crotch, she's not buying it. The fabric must breathe, after all. The mere mention of a thong is rejected with a grimace and the question, "How can that possibly be comfortable?" Growing up, you're bound to white cotton briefs. They are the Catholic girl's modern-day chastity belt.

If your father had his way, he would bring back the chastity belts of yesteryear. Nobility used these misogynistic devices to keep their prized possessions (read: their women) under lock and key. We realize that, in some kinky circles, a chastity belt is used to tantalize, but Daddy Dearest isn't looking at it that way. He sees a simple and effective way to protect his baby's jewels. This is just about all there is to say about Catholic dads. You think mom was buttoned up? All you need to know about pops is that he wants you to stay celibate, even when you're married, because no man will ever be good enough for his little girl.

Child's Play

Top (mis)communications about sex

Sexual lore is perpetuated at playgrounds, at sleepovers and around the neighborhood. And it's not just the bad kid in class who spreads the gossip. Sometimes it's a trusted friend.

We've heard enough misnomers over the years from fellow girls to make us scared, confused and laugh ourselves silly. Girls who once believed that pregnancy was something they could catch from dry humping, third base, public toilets and more are a dime a dozen.

Consider this urban legend: A woman who never knew she was pregnant or how she became pregnant suddenly delivered a baby in a bathtub. And if you don't believe us, ask our friend Chrissy, whose cousin was neighbors with a woman whose goddaughter had a college roommate who survived such a feat. She was forevermore known as "that girl."

Our favorite is the young lass who believed a woman became pregnant when she was lying in bed with a man she loved and his sperm climbed out of his penis, crawled across the bed and entered her vagina. Hey, at least she knew about sperm!

Myths about how *not* to get pregnant begin to top the charts as a girl grows older (but none the wiser). Here are our six faves:

You can't get pregnant if . . .

1. You use Saran Wrap on his schlong.
2. You rinse yourself immediately afterward with [insert here: Coca-Cola, Mountain Dew, fresh spring water].
3. You keep your clothes on (undone, but on).
4. You have sex standing up and remain standing straight up for an hour following the act.
5. You pee immediately after.
6. It's your first time.

Where the Boys Are

Boys—largely responsible for creating and fostering the "you can't get pregnant" myths as fodder for entry into your sacred land—had their own set of confusions to deal with above and beyond the lies they told. Ludicrous rumors of masturbation's menacing side effects (hairy palms and blindness) were created to scare boys stiff. We were brought to near tears of laughter when we asked a group of guys in a bar to recount other childhood sexual misunderstandings.

Eddie recalled how amazed he was that lube jobs were advertised on TV. It was only later, after several run-ins with burly mechanics, that he realized his mistake and figured out that lube jobs were much easier—and often much cheaper—to come by than blowjobs. Carlos remembered how sure he had been as a fifth-grader that the girls who dangled upside down from the jungle gym on the playground were the school sluts. This clearly was a chick's secret code for wanting sex. And, of course, he believed these gals smelled of fish.

"Well, for me," his friend Nick said with a smile, "the most obvious delusion I harbored was that girls peed out of their butts. You see, I had a younger brother—no sisters. He and I had the same parts. How else could a girl possibly pee except out her butt? Even worse was when there was dew left on the swings at recess. Surely, this was some sort of girl mucus. If you were the unlucky third-grade boy who forgot to flip the seat before swinging, you literally were marked for the rest of the day. It was traumatic to believe that you sat in 'girl potion' leaked from your cootie-filled classmate. Later on, as we became wiser in the ways of women, we all

WordPlay

Pee-pee
Childhood euphemism for both male and female genitalia.

came to know, love and pursue with some fervor real girl potion."

Perhaps our favorite belief—and also the strongest—came from a young man who learned all about sex from Swedish erotica. Jason and Pat were best friends in junior high. On a lark, they swiped a tape from the porn collection of a friend's mom(!). After successfully skipping out of school, they skateboarded back to Pat's house to make popcorn, settle in and learn, finally, what sex was all about. Thrilled, ecstatic and now clearly the coolest kids at Midland Junior High, Jason and Pat returned to school by lunchtime to share their new knowledge with the crew of waiting boys.

Something from the steamy scenes (remember, now, this *is* how our protagonist learned the basics) stuck with Jason until well into his late teens: "I'm going to be hung like a horse one day, like the guys in those flicks, and be able to pleasure beautiful women for at least an hour at a time." As the years passed and puberty ensued, he noticed that one particular growth spurt was not turning out quite as he had imagined. And so, Jason, now 31, still laments the shattered dreams of what could have been his sexual destiny.

"The first problem for all of us, men and women, is not to learn but to unlearn."

—Gloria Steinem

Catholic Schoolgirls Rule

Navigating a sea of sex myths is difficult enough. At some point, high-school boys are confounded by yet another mystery—the Catholic schoolgirl. Our Jewish friend Evan recalls a first date:

"Growing up, we had a number of Catholic schools in our area, but the girls may as well have attended class at the Vatican as far as my friends and I were concerned. How should we know the difference between Sacred Heart and Saint Bernadette's? What we knew was what we saw, and that was limited. Sacred Heart students sported the sexiest uniforms, and Saint Bernadette girls were rumored to be the easiest in the Midwest.

"Everything else we knew about Catholic girls we had learned from two questionable sources: parochial-school boys and the movies. The guys we knew from basketball camp either acted indifferently about their sister schoolmates or sang praises of the wildest things they would do. We didn't believe anything they said. But the movies certainly fed our imagination. Truthfully, even at 16 we knew the flicks were unfortunately more fiction than reality. Catholic schoolgirls remained a great mystery. For all we knew, they might as well have been unicorns: beautiful mythical creatures so elusive to man as to drive him crazy.

"When I was introduced to Meghan, a junior from Sacred Heart, I was petrified. When I landed a date with her, my terror—and excitement—intensified. My friends were ecstatic. They tested my coolness, gave me pointers, role-played mock scenarios.

"On date night, I picked up Meghan, met her parents and drove to the movies. Afterward we got some ice cream. I returned her safely home at 11 p.m. for curfew and even managed a kiss goodnight.

"The next day, my answering machine was jammed with a ton of messages: 'What was she like?' 'How did she smell?' 'Did she do magic tricks?' After cautiously relating that the date was even more normal than I had hoped, my friend James asked in desperation for the truth: 'Did she turn cartwheels, or was she bendy? Listen, were there gymnastics of any kind involved?'

"Finally, keeping the real truth hidden deep down, I embellished to appease the group and my own ego. I told them that we didn't go all the way but that she was totally into messing around in a way public-school girls just aren't. Now the expert, I explained that these seemingly untouchable girls' lack of day-to-day contact with boys had the opposite effect of what their parents might have intended. They were actually pros. I never had it so good."

SSL—Sex as a Second Language

When a guy asks you to *butter his bread*, you'll need to be prepared. Is he really looking for the Land O Lakes, or is he hoping for another sweet treat? Here is our edited list of euphemisms to improve your slang vocab. A word a day will get you on your way.

Sex, all varieties
Achieving congress
Banana split
Bed and breakfast
Boinking
Boning
Boom boom
Buzzing the honey hole
Churning butter
The deed
Doing the nasty
Donating to the
    missionary
Getting some
Getting your rocks off
Giving her the business
Going all the way
Hide the salami
Horizontal bone dance
Hot beef injection
It
Knockin' boots/uglies
Making love
Nookie
Nooner
Poking
Porking
Slamming
The sword in the stone
Taking the skin boat to
    tuna town
Two-backed beast

Oral sex, male
and female
BJ
Carpet cleaning
Chowing bird/box
Eating at the Y

Giving head
Going downtown
Having a box lunch
Hummer
Kneel at the altar
Lickety-split
Making Johnnie Walker red
Muff diving
Performing the big one
Playing the skin flute
Satisfying King Solomon
Speaking in tongues
Spelunking
Sucking the salami
Sweet smell of success

Penis

Bratwurst
Cannoli
Cherry splitter
Cock-a-doodle-doo
Dickie
The general
Giggle stick
Harry hot dog
Hot rod
Johnson
Love whistle
Master of ceremonies

Member
Odie
One-eyed snake
Pecker
Prick
Purple-headed monster
Russell the love muscle
Schlong
Shaft
Unit
Wanker
Weiner dog

Vagina

Bearded clam
Beaver
Bermuda triangle
Chinchilla
Cooch
Cooter
Fur burger
Garfield
Juice box
The juicy rough
Muff pie
Pearl
Pink lips
Puki
Pussy cat
Snatch

Squ'
Str
Twa.
Yum-yun.

Breasts

Bazongas
Bazookas
Bodacious tatas
Boobies
Boobs
Bosoms
Cupcakes
Enchiladas
Fun bags
Gagas
Headphones
Hooters
Knobs
Knockers
Mammies
Melons
Nips
Peepers
Pointer sisters
Sweater puffs
Teats
Tetons
Tits
Twins

"Some graffiti was once observed that said 'sex is good.'
All available evidence, however, points to the contrary."

—Matt Groening

Did Your Mom and Sister Agnes Teach You Enough?

By now, you've likely solved many of your miscommunication issues and learned, for better or worse, what sex is really all about. And, though you still may pine for the innocence of youth, you are now at least aware that women *can* get pregnant from having sex and that they most decidedly *cannot* get pregnant from a toilet seat.

You may wonder: "Didn't *everyone* have a lack of education in the ways of down there? Is it really just a Catholic thing?" Your answer awaits you: Measure your early teachings against the sex education afforded some more secularly minded "regular kids" with this simple quiz:

1. True or false: Sex education in health class consisted of diagrams of both the female *and* male genitalia.
2. True or false: Health class included the use of at least two of the following words: penis, condom, intercourse, birth control.

Bible Pop Quiz

Which of the following was *not* a passionate couple in the Bible?

    a.   Sarah and Abraham
    b.   Ruth and Boaz
    c.   Zipporah and Moses
    d.   Siegfried and Roy

Answer: d

3. True or false: You were allowed to ask anonymous questions *and actually have them answered* in health class.
4. True or false: Your parents told you about sex.
5. True or false: Your parents' big sex talk with you involved a red-faced mom who wanted to wash your mouth out with soap and water for mentioning such unmentionables.

The Regular Kids' Answers:

1. True. (They actually drew them on the chalkboard.)
2. True. (Health class wasn't always about menstruation and tampons.)
3. True. (When someone asked, "What does it actually *feel* like?" the teacher did not respond, "I wouldn't know yet.")
4. True. (Can you believe it?!)
5. False. (Huh? You've got to be kidding. But we're not! There are moms and dads who actually sit down and answer your sex questions. And some even give you condoms, just in case.)

Sibling Psychology

Your sister, not Sister, and your born-and-bred bodyguard

It's too bad that mom, dad and classmate Jane turned out to be such disappointments when it came to a little sexual learning. No problem, we Catholic girls just need to turn to our older, wiser siblings to get the juice, right? Maybe not. Read on for the further complications created by Catholic brothers and sisters. You only-children just might feel blessed.

Just the Girls

Older sisters are role models to be reckoned with. Growing up, when she wore acid wash, you wore acid wash. When she got a perm, you begged for a body wave. You hid under her bed to find out all about boys and kissing. You thought you would learn everything from her, but surprise, surprise, older sisters are often just as tight-lipped as their matriarchs. Catholic sisters don't spew details. You may have been blessed with a big sis who actually talked shop. Consider yourself lucky.

As the sheltered little sister, you had to be selective with your sex questions. Once you hit your not-so-sweet sixteen, you finally mustered the courage to ask her: "When did you lose your virginity?" One would think that this is a pretty straightforward question. No way. Catholic Sister Craftiness took over. The gist: she lied.

When answering the young lass's inquiry, an older sister will bump up her did-it date just enough years to ensure her younger, copycat sister will wonder if she is ready to have sex herself. But not too many years to make it seem that sex is undoable or unallowable. She said 20 when she should have said 17 because she didn't want you to go at it at 16. (And, to be honest, you probably would have.) So you believed what sister said but did it anyway.

Oh, Brother

Like dads, there's not much to discuss when it comes to discussing it with big bro. The bottom line? He speaks softly and carries a big stick. He will use his Louisville Slugger to break the knees of anyone who touches his baby sister.

WordPlay

Müssentouch

German-American vagina.

WordPlay

Punani

Italian-American vagina.

Don't Tell Mom But . . .

When a Catholic girl grows up a bit, she realizes the need to keep certain lines of communication open with a sibling, even with a don't-ask-don't-tell one. Someone has to know where you're *really* spending the night. Commonly shared secrets include:

1. I'm ditching Retreat for a hotel room.
2. My boyfriend's folks are out of town.
3. My boyfriend drives a van.
4. I went on the Pill.
5. I gave my boyfriend a key to my pad.
6. I'm living with my boyfriend.
7. My boyfriend lost his job.
8. I'm pregnant.
9. I'm a lesbian.
10. I'm writing a self-help book about Catholic girls and sex.

Bible Pop Quiz

According to Colossians, 3:18 what is a woman's sexual role?
   a. Subservient: Women were created to serve and satisfy men's sexual desires.
   b. Balanced: Women were created to pleasure both men and themselves equally, in cases of procreation.
   c. Dominant: Women were created to teach men about sexuality.
   d. Utilitarian: Women were created to bear children.

Answer: a

Confessional Etiquette
Talking to the clergy

Talking to your priest after your eventual sex acts (see chapters 3 and 4) can be just as nerve-racking as dealing with your parents. "Bless me, Father, for I have . . ." Are you really going to do this? Are you going to confess your sexual sins to a man who has taken a vow to denounce the very act you seek to confess? Forget *disapproving.* He can't even relate. Why not give him a couple of average sins and pray forgiveness directly to God later for the biggies? But wait! That's not the Catholic way. You must get absolution. You must confess. Oh, yes. But you can't. Yes, you must. No. Yes.

Here's the thing: You need forgiveness. You, as a Catholic, vow to avoid the near occasion of sin. And remember, if it's not for making babies, even making out is out. If you are walking around with blemishes on your moral record—and, ahem, sexual scars at that—you're a living-and-breathing damned soul doomed for life in purgatory, or worse. You need to confess. You need to confess as often as necessary and as often as possible. Hey, if for no other reason, it gets rid of the guilt. After all, if Monsignor O'Shea says you're absolved, you're good to go.

When confessing, keep in mind that the sacrament of penance takes the three Cs: commitment, concentration and craftiness. *Commitment:* You are resolved to receive absolution. You know what you did was wrong, and you won't do it again (until the next time). *Concentration:* This is hard, this is embarrassing, this seems out of your league. Use a simple, mind-numbing distraction to make it easier to get out what you need to say. Take a lesson from your guy friends and think about baseball. (To prolong their prowess in bed, they think batters and pitchers and useless stats on the inside, while touching boobies on the outside.) *Craftiness:* There is a time and a place to talk sex. Since a confessional stall just seems wrong anytime, follow our tips for how to accomplish the task with the least amount of fallout.

Sex-Confessional Know-how

1. Go to a new priest.
2. Go to a different parish.
3. Never go face-to-face.
4. Never, ever go face-to-face with Father I-wish-you-weren't-a-Father.
5. Find an old priest with a hearing aid.
6. Keep it simple: Don't divulge details.

When all is said and done, say your Hail Marys and Our Fathers, and say them twofold. You probably simplified the truth while you were in the box, so make up for it outside the box. Follow our handy penance chart for solutions to all your sexual situations.

"One cannot really be a Catholic and grown up."
—George Orwell

WordPlay

Spumoni

An Italian ice cream having different layers of colors and flavors, often containing fruit and nuts.

The Penance Chart

	The Boyfriend for a Year	The We-Just-Started-Dating Guy
FIRST BASE	Aw, shucks, you're pure with the pucker.	1 Hail Mary.
SECOND BASE	1 Glory be to the Father.	Donation to the poor box.
THIRD BASE	1 Hail Mary, 2 Our Fathers.	Get your hands dirty helping in the church garden.
ORAL SEX	Light a candle at church.	10 Hail Marys, 4 Our Fathers.
SEX MISSIONARY	8 Hail Marys, 2 Our Fathers.	18 Hail Marys, 8 Our Fathers and an Act of Contrition.
KINKY STUFF	Head up church bake sale.	Full rosary, within 24 hours.

Note: When it comes to your hubby, you're in the clear (sort of) as long as you don't use condoms, cervical caps, spermicides, diaphragms, sponges, pills . . .

If you just can't face your priest, try a little self-absolution home remedy. Follow our redemptive guide. Buyer beware: This oh-so-scientific chart might not be accepted by Saint Peter at the Pearly Gates.

The We're-Just-Friends Guy	The I-Can't-Believe-I-Finally-Had-My-Chance-to-Be-with-Him Guy	The I-Think-Your-Name-Is-Lisa-When-It's-Really-Laura Guy
Put your mouth to good use and read to the blind.	Go to the longer choir Mass.	Hey, kissing bandit, offer a prayer to the souls in purgatory (and your own).
A bedside prayer.	9 Hail Marys and read all of *Genesis*.	15 Hail Marys, 2 Our Fathers.
Recite the Apostle's Creed twice.	12 Hail Marys, 6 Our Fathers and no meat on Friday.	Full rosary.
20 Hail Marys, 10 Our Fathers	Volunteer at the soup kitchen for a month.	Two full rosaries, plus a trip to Grandma's house.
25 Hail Marys, 14 Our Fathers and a prayer in Latin.	Full rosary, in church on Sunday morning.	Go directly to church, do not pass go, do not collect $200, pray the day away.
Full rosary immediately after the act.	A weekend retreat of repenting.	There's no hope. call your local convent —we don't have all the answers.

God Times

The communicative forecast may seem bleak, but for some Catholics there is a silver lining. Listen to Kelly's hopeful story:

"I was home from campus on summer break when my parents went to golf camp in South Carolina for a week. Naturally, I had a party. My boyfriend stayed overnight—a bigger taboo under the 'rents' roof than drunk college kids. I thought I did a bang-up cleanup job: The cans were safely recycled, the spills were killed and the carpet footprints were carefully vacuumed away.

"The next day, I got home from my summer job and found mom in the kitchen. 'How was your trip?' I asked. She continued to scour the counter. No looks, no response. My stomach dropped and my guilt-meter ran high. What had I done? Confused, I went to my bedroom. I found the answer on my night table. White-faced, I nearly threw up when I read those fatal words: GLAD YOU HAD A GOD [purposeful misspelling?] TIME WHILE WE WERE AWAY. Placed alongside the note was a tiny, ripped-off corner of a LifeStyles condom wrapper. I guessed that piece of the packaging had fallen in a crack of the sheets. My mom had stripped my bed to wash the linens and WHAM! found the my-daughter-is-having-sex evidence.

"Utterly distressed, I paced my room with the understanding that downstairs my mother KNEW, actually had PROOF, of my sexual exploits. I had always guessed she assumed we had done it, because Kevin and I had been together for years. But assumption and confirmation are two different things. Sex finally stared my mom in the face, and all she could do was scrub the house.

"For days I faced the supreme silent treatment. There was no eye contact. Grunts replaced speech. I felt like a criminal. Eventually she began to act normal. She internalized and she ignored.

"Ten years later, my mom and I were having dinner while dad perfected his swing at Pebble Beach. Two bottles of wine in the hole, we began to joke about teenage years and the stupid things I had thought were oh-so-smart. We even talked about the time I got caught when I was home from college. I couldn't believe it. We had spent the past decade avoiding the word *sex*, and here was my mom talking about the big condom-wrapper bust. She finally addressed sex for the first time. 'You'll never get a guy to marry you if you give up the goods too soon,' she said. The whole chat was brief, not even ten minutes. But I finally had my sex talk—it only took thirty years."

Chapter Three

The Deed

Sacred acts: Making the decision and
planning the day

We Catholic girls are quite the conundrum. There are scores of urban legends about the ladies behind the gates who, without testosterone in their daily school life, become wild and unruly sexual beasts. Getting an invitation to a Catholic-school dance became the chance of a lifetime for a public-school boy. On the flip side, there are iconographic images of pious petticoats who obey both fathers—the heavenly and the household. An invitation to Sunday night's spaghetti dinner is the closest a public-school boy is going to get. And then there are modern Catholic girls who live adeptly in both worlds. They enjoy sex. A lot. But they feel bad about it. Really bad.

So here's where we get down to the dirty. From stepping up to the plate to rounding the bases and hitting a homer, this chapter outlines the stats, the sass and the down-low lowdown on Catholic girls and sex.

"Some men love oral sex. . . . If you find a man like this, treat him well. Feed him caviar and don't let your girl-friends catch a glimpse of him."

—Cynthia Heimel

Everything But . . .

Fun with foreplay

You may remember your first kiss sweetly, fondly even, but also we bet with a smile. It may have been like Liz's, who forgot her breath mints at a spin-the-bottle game. Or like Caroline's, whose boyfriend instructed her to stop making perfect, speedy circles with her tongue. Or it may have been like Melinda's (yes, the co-author), whose first tongue kiss produced enough saliva to end a drought. The first kiss was an innocent foray into foreplay—the pecks, the pokes, the pets that pave the way to sex.

Heavy Petting

Just kissing doesn't last long. We're guessing your teenage Romeo tried to feel you up by the second make-out session. He fumbled with your bra, hastening the hoorah. Regardless, fondling your little buds didn't do much for you, anyway. You prayed for bigger boobs, you even tried a chocolate-milk diet. Hopefully, your current love has mastered the one-handed unhooking and you finally have filled out the C cup you dreamed of. OK, at least you manage a B. All right, so you buy an A. . . .

Finger Blasting and Hand Jobs

Pretty soon he starts to get handsy. The potential problem? To that teenage Romeo, the more the merrier. It's all about how many digits he can cram in. If that's not bad enough, now it's time to reciprocate with a hand job. Your biggest fear? He's been doing it to himself for years, so how can you possibly top his technique?

Dry Humping

It may be fantastic for you—you may even have had your first orgasm. But your guy complains of more side effects than a bottle of pain reliever: Chafing, soreness, burning and aches top the list. (Why do you think they are always going for the real deal?)

Oral Sex

There are two different camps concerning the sin factor of oral sex. If you're part of the first, you think anything but intercourse is fine. Case-study Sandy: "Blowjobs never bothered me shamefully like sex did. They're a part of life, and I think, 'What's the fun if you don't share?'" As for the second camp, you think playing the skin flute or having your guy go downtown is even more intimate than intercourse itself. You would rather spread your legs than your lips, so you preserve it for Mr. You-Better-Be-Right.

Let's ponder the age-old debate: To spit or to swallow? On the one hand, spitting lessens the guilt-blow by sparing you a dose of love juice. On the other hand, if you have bad aim, spitting can be just plain sticky. And let's not even dis-

WordPlay

Sloppy seconds

1. Going out with your buddy's ex-gal/guy.

2. Hooking up with a guy who already has hooked up earlier in the evening. (Usage: "I just hooked up with Ted!" "So did I like an hour ago. Girl, you got sloppy seconds!")

3. Second base using tongue.

4. An endless debate of definition.

cuss the grodie taste. If you're swift in your swallowing, however, the flavor won't linger (not to mention all that protein helps for a nice shiny head of hair). Plus, you literally eat your evidence so there's no need for cover-up. The con? The evil stays within you for a full digestive cycle. It's twenty-four hours before you're completely guilt-free.

You Can Leave Your Hat On

Kerry was ready for foreplay. She wasn't ready for the surprises she got from her multi-culti beaus.

"When I was 16 I went on a cruise in Europe with my best friend, Heather, and her family. In each port, the cruise director set the teenagers up with local kids for social events. While we were on the French Riviera, I had a boyfriend named Jean-Luc. He could barely speak English, but he was so hot. At Movie Night, we sat in the back and I almost gave him a hand job, but freaked out when I saw his penis. It looked like it was wearing a little skin turtleneck. It was OFFENSIVE. I fled. Heather explained that it was uncircumcised, but as far as I was concerned, it was untouchable. I was free from him and his skin flap just as we set sail for Barcelona.

"For the next three years, I would only date Jewish guys. Better safe than sorry, I thought. Until . . .

"Junior year of college, I studied abroad in Bologna and met Luca. Before I could even think about his sheath status, I was in love. I took a chance and went for his uncircumcised member. Much to my surprise, it wasn't the disgusting deed I thought it would be. Everything was so much easier. It took half the time, half the effort. I basically held my hand there and let the skin do the rest. Less work, more yay. From then on, I couldn't get enough of still-encased salami and haven't dated a Jewish guy since."

The Pros and Cons of a Catholic Partner

In all honesty, your first might not even be a good Catholic boy. But if you think keeping it in the church-blazer crowd might lesson the blow, there are certain things to consider.

Pro: Your mother will trust him to take you out on dates.
Con: Your mother will trust him to take you out on dates.
Pro: He'll understand your ambiguity and shame regarding sex.
Con: He'll understand your ambiguity and shame regarding sex, and he'll use that knowledge to employ the perfect lines to persuade you to have lots of sex.
Pro: He won't take sex lightly.
Con: He won't take birth control seriously.
Pro: He goes to church.
Con: You'll see him at church.

WordPlay

Third-ish base

A reputation maker. A guy says he got to third to make it seem like he got a blowjob; a girl makes it seem like she only gave a hand job.

Blowjob

Brain surgery.

Cashing in Your V-Card

How to know when the time is right

At some point, all the foreplay becomes forgettable, and you think you're ready. But you're not sure. Your whole life you've been told sex is a sin. After months of messing around, you just don't buy it—eternal damnation be damned. In the end, there may never be a perfect time to take the love train. "I wasn't really ready for sex," Annabelle told us. "Sex was ready for me." Don't fret, you'll find the right schedule for you.

Below you'll find some of the most prevalent reasons (for better or worse) that girls go all the way.

Dropping the L-Bomb

Love. The first and most essential reason is simply being in love. As a general rule, you should wait until he drops the L-bomb before you agree to release the missiles. In dire circumstances, if you think you hear a garbled "love" under his breath, it can be considered a bomb drop. However, it does not count if he utters the word in the middle of making love.

And for you post-virginal vixens who still find it hard to legitimize being with a new beau (you're not sure if he's special enough and, dare we say, sacred enough), take a lesson from our friend Maureen: "To this day, I still can't have sex with someone unless I think I love him. But who knows? I'm single and I'm horny. Maybe it's just changing the definition a bit. Like, 'I *love* your blue eyes.' "

The Time Factor

You've been together long enough that even *you* are bored of straight-up hooking up. Everyone assumes you've been together *that way*, anyway. Your friends keep asking, "Have you done it, have you done it, you should really do it, why haven't you done it?" And they're right, you think. It must be time.

Everybody's Doing It

It may sound silly, but many girls cite this as a reason for first-time sex. Consider Jenny: "I was such a good girl in high school. I was such a prude. I only hooked up. I never had sex. When I got to college, I told myself I didn't want to be a virgin anymore. I told myself it wasn't a sin. If good girls like Vanessa and Maryanne were doing it, then maybe it was high time I did as well."

Ready, Set, Go

You may know these girls; you may even have been one of them. You just know you're ready to have sex. You likely aren't a Catholic.

Are You Ready to Do It?

You think you're ready, but, like any indecisive Catholic girl, you're having second thoughts. You're letting your horniness and your conscience duke it out. Answer true or false to the following questions, and see if it's right to feel all right for the first time or the not-so-first time.

1. I love him.
2. I'm pretty sure I love him.
3. He will hold me afterward.
4. He'll stop if I say it hurts.
5. We plan on using contraception other than *coitus interruptus*.
6. We have talked about where to get contraception.
7. My best friend likes him.
8. I wouldn't be embarrassed to tell my friends.
9. He doesn't kiss and tell. (You just know.)
10. I know he's been tested.
11a. For first-timers: He knows I'm a virgin.
11b. For already-active girls: He's OK with my lucky number.

He's the One

You're sure he's the guy for you. It's easy enough to evaluate if he's sexworthy. Follow our simple checklist:

- You are OK with remembering his name forever.
- You can gab with him like he's a gal pal.
- If it doesn't work out, and you never talk again, you probably won't regret it.
- You've spoken with him about protection.

12. He knows my mother's first name.
13. He knows about the embarrassing birthmark on my bum.
14. He calls me his girlfriend.
15. He has a job.
16. He has a car.
17. I won't hate myself in the morning. (Trick question: Catholics *always* regret it in the morning.)
18. I really want to do it. At least he knows my name.

Scoring

Mostly true:
Honey, there is no time like the present. You seem to understand the importance of weighing your decisions. You are ready for some boots-a-knockin'.

Mostly false:
If you go through with it, you'll likely endure a season of repenting. So don't do it until you find a fellow who can turn your falses into trues.

Catholic Schoolboy Suitors

Here's a glimpse of Catholic wooers better left to their own devices.

The "I Might Have the Calling" Catholic

These pious guys might seem appealing at first for their devotion, kindness and sheer points-with-mom factor. Be warned: These Soldiers of Christ are on their way to a relationship with Mary that can't be tampered with.

The "Super Guido" Catholic

Your Super Guido loves his mother, loves the Church, but *really* loves cruisin' in his Dodge Viper. He can name every line from the *Godfather* trilogy and *Goodfellas*. We're not saying Italian-Americans make bad partners. Hardly. We're merely suggesting you avoid the white patent-leather version.

The "A-Little-Too-Irish" Catholic

He's got a lot of friends and always knows where the party's at—usually in his basement. Now, we don't mean to imply that *all* Irish boys are bound to beer, but *some* green-isle guys prefer getting sauced rather than *saucy* with their girl.

wire-rimmed glasses favored by the 65-year-old set

seems far more comfortable than the other boys in a buttoned-up collar

leather-bound prayer book

report card: an A for every subject except religion, which garners an A+

black dress socks only

I Might Have the Calling

Did he actually *bathe* in Drakkar Noir?

clearly using styling products for the wet look

shirt unbuttoned as low as possible, revealing some chest hair, an Italian horn, a crucifix and a Saint Anthony medal

Is that a pinky ring?

the shiniest shoes in class—faux Gucci loafers to boot!

Super Guido

parents' vacation itinerary with scribbled additions, including: 1) phone number and directions to Kelsey's house for Saturday night party; 2) call Tony, Todd, Casey; 3) swipe weekly missal for went-to-church proof; 4) make sure Mad Dog's bro gets pony keg

red wine-stained lips; he took an unauthorized swig from the goblet of Communion wine, again

sports bottle filled with Southern Comfort and Coke; drool-stained religion notebook littered with pot leaves; cough medicine for emergency drink only—Roboshots; on-vacation O'Byrne's house keys; street signs from corner of Ridgeway and Olentangy

lunch: leftovers from Sunday night's spaghetti and meatball dinner; grandma slipped a $20 in the bag.

puke-scented Guinness T-shirt lifted from older brother

cuts and scrapes from a routine night of boozing and street spills

A-Little-Too-Irish

Giddyap Partner

How to parley with the fellas

You think you've picked out the right chap, but how do you have the sex chat? Given the lack of communication we received from our spiritual and parental leaders, it's easy to see how so many of us modern Catholic girls have grown up without the ability to broach the subject without fleeing in a fit of embarrassment. So how are we to know the best ways to (gulp) approach the topic with the chosen one?

Talking about sex is not an easy thing for *anyone*. But whether it's your first time or forty-first time, communicating with your partner is necessary. For one, as adept as we are at denial, sex is much better if you're able to talk about it (or so we've been told by our girlfriends). Here we give tips for the novice and also the seasoned expert.

Spicing Up Your Sex Life

You feel mushy thinking about him. You think you may love him. You enjoy getting turned on by him. But really you want to get nasty. How do you let him know you've got real, big-girl fantasies when you can barely admit them to yourself?

Just like a boy scout, be prepared. Know what you want before you speak. Remember how you learned your rosary? You recited it over and over as quickly as possible. Figure out what you're going to say, practice it in front of a mirror a few times, rehearse it in the shower and then meditate on it. Pray it. Repeat it over and over. That way, when the moment arrives, your guy will hear it as you rehearsed it. Or at least you won't fumble out something along the lines of, "Durr. Duh. Um. Sex! HAH! Anyway . . ."

Here's one way your Catholicism can help you. Once you're ready to delve into the truth about your desires with that special someone, conjure up all your repression into one nice and neat pure little package. Use your secret shame to your advantage. Say, "I'm nervous. I'm innocent. I don't know how to talk about this. . . ." This is very sexy talk for your man. It says to him, "Guide me, show me, teach me, big boy." Of course, once you've "learned" from your man, there's no stopping you from going wild and even teaching him a thing or two. He'll feel like it was all his doing. Once the conversation kicks things off, there are no boundaries in a healthy relationship.

If you prefer a tactic that doesn't scream naive, or if your man already knows enough about you not to buy the innocent act, try one of these opening lines:

- "I couldn't imagine talking to anyone else about this."
- "I just never felt this turned on. It makes me want to explore more."
- "I wish I could be doing more for you."
- "I can't believe I'm admitting this to you, but you make me feel really sexy when you . . ."
- "Dude, we *need* to have a sex talk or no more sex!"

When to Be a Silent Partner

Although healthy adult relationships involve frank discussion, there are times when you should heed your Catholic shame and keep your lips sealed. Here's the first and only firm rule to keeping your mouth shut: *Don't say a word when the subject of past loves comes up*. It doesn't matter if you and your former guy shared only kisses. Your new guy may say, "Come on, I'm not jealous," or he may share unsolicited details about *his* previous girlfriends. Trust us. Don't go there. No matter how together a guy seems, he's reduced to nothing once he contemplates the truth about his lady's past.

There is one exception to the keep-our-pasts-locked-in-the-closet rule. The relationship's over and it's over for good. Perhaps you've had your fill and are ready to send him packing, or maybe you've walked in on him with your would-be maid of honor. Then you can tell. You can tell the whole truth. *And* you can embellish.

Variations on a Theme

It's here that we thought we'd first give you some tips about approaching partners of other religions. What nuances would a sexually savvy girl need to know to make it with a Jew or a Protestant? We wondered how an atheist or a Buddhist might respond to a Catholic girl's particular sexual hang-ups. After talking to dozens of men from all faiths, we realized an important truth. There are only two types of men you will ever encounter as a Catholic girl: Catholics and non-Catholics.

Catholic guys, though appealing for the mom approval factor, actually have more difficult psyches to navigate for us Catholic girls. For one thing, your Irish, Italian, Polish or Hispanic lover probably has his own unique brand of childhood Catholic luggage. Perhaps he's still ashamed of his own dirty fantasies. He might feel tremendous pangs of guilt having sex with a woman he doesn't love. Or maybe he can't face a Catholic girl who has had previous partners without thinking that she's slutty. Regardless, Catholic shame isn't reserved for us girls, and it's likely that your man will harbor some, too.

For another thing, they get us. They know us. Their sisters and cousins and first girlfriends are just like us. This introduces two potential problems: 1) There can be no trickery or secrets, since we are not mysteries to them. They did not learn about Catholic girls from watching porn. And 2) They, more than anyone else we know, are looking for that elusive feminine combination: the saint on their arm and the slut in their bed. They want their mom for a wife and the most popular girl from the whorehouse on the hill for a lover. They're intimate with the idea of sainthood, and they, too, have been running scared from the devil since baptism. That's a lot to live up to.

As for your non-Catholic partners, you can do very little wrong here. They see us as some sort of spectacle—a forbidden treasure trove of their wild imaginations. As a result, we have an opportunity to take control. That's right, *control*. We can create a persona and go with it. So, if you want to take things slowly, it's chalked up to a "Catholic thing." And if you want to be wild, well, it's also chalked up to that Catholic thing.

The only booby trap here is expressing too early in your relationship your desire to marry in the faith, in the House of the Lord, and to baptize your kids—all with saints' names. Save this until the date is set or the baby is on the way. (Note: For many, the baby on the way is exactly *when* the date is set. Again, it can be chalked up to a "Catholic thing.")

Top Catholic Guy Come-on Lines

In High School
1. "Please, please, please."
2. From the star student in Italian class: *"Voglio avere sesso con ti, per favore, per favore, per favore."*
3. "Everything is going to be fine. Trust me."
4. "Did you know we beat Saint Michael's last night?"
5. "Let's test out my new waterbed."
6. "Aren't you curious? Come on. Please." (See number 1 for continued begging.)

The College Years
1. "Do you like jazz?"
2. "I don't have much experience with coeducation. Do you think you could help me adjust?"
3. Handing the lady a bottle of champagne: "Drink this until you're naked."
4. While studying abroad: "I've got a surprise for you—condoms from America."
5. "What time should I set the alarm for?"
6. "Please, please, please."

Post-Graduation
1. "Hi, I'm _____."
2. "I work with kids."
3. "I just got Ashes."
4. "I want to . . ." (insert here: "be in you," "feel you around me," "do bad things to you.")
5. "No games, no jokes, no lines. You're coming home with me right now."
6. "Please, please, please."

Roving Reporter

There comes a time in most people's lives when they take that plunge into the forbidden sea. Sometimes they drown. Sometimes they swim. But either way, it's man overboard. "When did *you* fall from grace?"

Vincent Kelly, 50
Married with ten kids

"I like to call him Patrick, my first son."

Jimmy McCracken, 15
Fordham Prep sophomore

"My hot babysitter, Tiffany, and I went at it when I was, like, 12. She was 17 and way into it."

Danny and Francesca Gallo, both 29
Newlyweds

Francesca answers for both:
"He lost it senior year in high school. I lost it sophomore year in college to my first love."
(In truth, Danny was a sophomore in college, while Francesca was entering her second year of Holy Child High School for Girls.)

Iris Sullivan, 65
Unmarried

> "I am still in the Lord's good graces, but if I knew then what I know now, I would have done it and done it some more."

Andrea Perez, 22
Recent college grad

> "Durr! Prom night, silly."

"Lead me not into temptation; I can find the way myself."

—Rita Mae Brown

Sexpectations

A girl for every reason

Girls' expectations of sex range tremendously. They define her sexual type. Read on for the typical pre-sex obsessions that mark different gals. And for the guys, get a glimpse of how this chick behaves.

The Philosopher

She's the girl who believes sex is going to be a profound, life-altering moment. She thinks it will be her monumental entrance into womanhood and her new role as a liberated lady. She knows the seriousness of sex, she's dealt with any hesitations and she decides to go for it anyway. She welcomes this significant step into the unknown and the physical union of two souls.

For the guys: She'll be sensitive, loving and generous during sex. She expects every time to be deep and mind-blowing. She also will probably be open to new experiences, but her kinky, wild quotient is definitely subdued.

The Realist

She says she's scared—she's sure it will hurt. She expects no pleasure and just wants to get it over with. The hurt factor is *huge* for her.

For the guys: Because her ouch element is so high, she may have lots of tension during the deed. But bear with her. She often ends up as the most vivacious of all the post-coital cuties. Why? Her expectations are so low that once it gets good, it gets really good.

The OCD (Obsessive Compulsive Disorder)

She can handle the pain; she just can't handle the blood. Rampant high-school legends of mortifying moments on bloodstained sheets contribute to her terror. She comes prepared with new linens and bleach lest she join the ranks of gossiped-about bleeders.

WordPlay

Sexpectations

1. Pre-sex obsessions that torment virgins.

2. The anxiety preceding a romp in the hay with a new fella.

For the guys: Though she might seem clinical, this gal simply needs to mop up the evidence of her first time. She grows up to be the girl who's quick with the post-coital cleanup. (Read: The sheets are changed the very next morning.)

The Modern Catholic

She believes she is going to be picked up by demons and dragged right to hell the second the seeds have been spilled. She thinks her mom is going to disown her and her father is never going to speak to her again. And her priest? Please. She can't even imagine ever being allowed back into her church. Her expectations are so dire that when she is in fact faced with normal next-day guilt, embarrassment and self-pity, a wave of relief passes over her. She vows never to sin again—at least until after suppertime.

For the guys: These are the girls who can really let go, letting you take the lead. The few moments following sex might be filled with regret, but rest assured: She'll be back as soon as she gets over this slip into sin. (Tip: Unsolicited, tell her she's a really good person.)

Boudoir Prayer

Matthew, Mark, Luke and John,
Bless this mattress we sex upon,
Help us sex with zeal and zest,
Help us sex our very best.

The Virgin Journal

We coerced Jessica to dig up her old high-school diary. In it, she details her less-than-perfect first time:

March 30

Dear Diary,

Big news: I am ready to have sex. Not tonight or anything, but I definitely want it to be with Chris AND before I leave for college. I also want it to be *really special,* so I am going to start planning it today.

Times to do it:

1. Easter vacation: Two full weeks off from stupid school to do it right.
2. My prom, when we'll definitely be spending the night in the same place.
3. His prom. Scratch that, I'll need my girls in close vicinity for right afterward.

Places to do it:

A hotel room would be very cool and very grown-up, I think. Also would be totally private. Definitely it will have to be in a hotel room.

Jessica

April 12

Dear Diary,

I told Chris that I want to have sex. I also told him that it HAS to be special, or I won't give it up. He was really psyched. I had to coax him into the hotel-room idea, because he doesn't see the point of laying out cash when we can do it

anywhere. Plus, he doesn't get why I would even need to wait until prom. But all in all he was really psyched.

So he booked a hotel room at the Hyatt, where my Evening Under the Stars prom will take place. YAY, I think. I hope it doesn't hurt. I hope he knows to bring me flowers and stuff. We should totally check in with one name like we're married!

J

May 1

Dear Diary,

Prom was a disaster. I am still a virgin.

We had the pre-prom party at our house. Mom and Dad let us have champagne. By the time we got to the dance, we were all a little tipsy. There was so much booze in the limo that Chris, Brad and Keith kept sneaking out to drink.

Everyone got really smashed at the hotel. Anyway, Chris was missing for like an hour, and I was getting antsy, so I decided to go to our private haven, slip out of my dress and wait for him. I found him there, lying facedown in a little puddle of puke. I had to sleep on the chair by the TV. When he finally woke up the next morning, he was so hungover, he could barely speak.

So now I have to wait all over again for the perfect moment to do it, and without a prom coming up I can't possibly imagine how we could make it special. I just hope Chris doesn't go nail some Saint Catherine's slut after I finally got the courage to do it.

Jess

May 12
1 DAY NV ! ! ! ! ! ! ! ! ! ! !
(not virgin)

Dear Diary,

I lost my virginity last night !
Kendra had people over. Chris and I went off to fool around, and before I knew it he was telling me how much he loved me and wanted me and how we didn't need a fancy-pants hotel room to "make love." We just needed each other. I didn't so much think up a response as just let it happen. And so we did it right there on Kendra's brother's old racing-car bed!!!!

Jessie

May 13
2 Days NV

Dear Diary,

Am pretty sure must be pregnant. Just feel it. I talked to Julie, she said she and Charlie used TWO condoms the first time. OMIGOD. We only used one. Am not going to flip out b/c love Chris soooo much and I believe we can work through anything. Will go to Church today and pray. Surely showing up when it's not Sunday must count for something.

Jessica, the future Mrs. Crerello

May 15
4 Days NV

Dear Diary,

Got my period. On Mother's Day.

J.A.M.

Not-so-Hot Spots

When reality bites

So you've made the decision, settled on the boy and now you need to set the rest. Most often there is less planning and more scrambling the day you decide to do it. First: the place. With time, the imagined setting for your first encounter slowly melts into reality. It was your childhood dream: You are in your beautiful white satin wedding gown. Your fella, dressed in a tux with top hat and tails, carries you over the threshold into your hotel room overlooking the deep blue Pacific. He slowly takes off your wedding gown, button by thousands of buttons. (Huh? We know it's the Catholic flight of fancy, but were you wearing the thing on the plane?) And finally you indulge in the wedded bliss of one another. It is magical. It is mystical. It is illusion.

By the time you're ready to do it, your dream honeymoon has faded, and you've settled for a hotel on the highway. Your handsome hunk of a date has gone to the room early and strewn rose petals on the bed. There are white tapered candles everywhere. There is a pleasant, aromatic smell. He has taken the liberty of hanging a tasteful and beautiful negligee in the closet. It is the most special night of your young life. Nah, it probably won't happen that way, either.

Most likely there won't be a plan at all. It will be a battle to elude parents, siblings, roommates and the police and find a solo spot. You may have to deflower in the car, in the den while your folks are out for the night, your friend's place while *her* parents are gone for the night or your triple in the dorm. Don't fret. Your first time can never be forgettable.

"Give me chastity and continence—but not yet."
—Saint Augustine

Where to Bare

The Catholic ideal: two virgins in a honeymoon suite. It was your parents' expectation and most likely your preteen dream. Reality: Most modern Catholic girls punctured their purity a little earlier than the wedding day and in a less romantic spot than a four-star hotel.

The Basement

For many Catholic gals, drawers dropping happened down under. The house, that is. Your parents were upstairs having dinner with the Walshes, while you and Mike made out to *Better Off Dead* downstairs. Before you could say ten Hail Marys, you were doing it. There was no time to think about it: It only lasted through the first "I want my $2" bike chase from the flick.

Down Under

1. Excuse for being with a boy in the basement.
2. Air-hockey table: good for flirtatious competition (he likely considered this foreplay).
3. Comfortable sectional sofa with afghan crocheted by grandma. Obvious spot of seduction.
4. Last year's Christmas cards collect dust next to sports trophies.
5. Laundry hamper filled with clean socks and underwear. Good for messy cleanups.
6. Mismatched patchwork pillow made in home ec for quick concealment of his manliness.
7. Old school pennants from Iona Prep, Notre Dame and Marymount.
8. Stocked with Glenlivet and vintage reds. He picked the lock to loosen things up.
9. Extra roll of toilet paper, for complete condom concealment.
10. Your older brother's old 49ers trashcan: condom disposal site.
11. Your St. Bernard, Sammy, sent down by mom to "check on you."
12. Poster-sized annual portraits of the whole family: They're watching!
13. Stack of old family records: Sinatra, Peter, Paul & Mary, Louis Prima, Johnny Mathis, Perry Como, John Denver, Linda McCartney, Carly Simon, the Righteous Brothers, the Beatles, *Purple Rain*, *Saturday Night Fever* and *Strawberry Shortcake's Berry Merry Christmas*. What's playing: Guns N' Roses tape.
14. Creak in third step alerted impending doom of parental arrival.
15. Point of evacuation in case of emergency. Cracked to prevent excessive steaming.

Sometimes the basement was only a breeding ground for boxes. First times happened in other less-than-perfect locales:

Local Hotel Room

A cheap hotel was a prom-night prerequisite for a lucky few. But it took money, means, masterminding and an older sibling's credit-card number.

The Family Wagon

It was the easiest for homebound honeys, but we hope you remembered to wipe down the windows. God forbid mom saw your fogged-up sweaty palm prints in the morning.

College Dorm

Maneuvering twin beds required real dexterity and good communication with roommate—no savvy single gal would use an '80s scrunchi as a signal on the door.

The Beach

Crashing waves certainly set the mood, but even the biggest blanket couldn't prevent sand in your pants.

Camp

Up against an old oak with David from the boys' camp sounded fun, if not splintery. Oh, wait, we Catholics never went to sleep-away; that's the modern Jewish girl's less-than-perfect place.

Fits Like a Glove
Your protection plan

There is one part of planning that cannot be overlooked—birth control. Let's be realistic here: You most likely haven't been timing your ovulation, and pulling out would be a real downer.

Unless you're already on the Pill (for cramps, of course), you'll need to get another form of birth control. Condoms are the safest and easiest way to get rid of the remains of the lay, when used properly. Don't rely on the guy. This is the same boy, after all, who thinks stealing fireworks is the *coolest*. If you're too bashful for the 7-Eleven, make a friend go. Steal them from your brother. Go to Planned Parenthood. Use the machine at the bowling alley. Wherever, whenever—just do it before the deed. You don't want something unplanned, do you?

WordPlay

Pulling Out Like a Good Catholic

Coitus interruptus.

Soda pop

A pregnancy-prevention urban legend that leaves the woman with a sticky vagina and a baby with a sweet tooth.

Time to Get Serious: Sexually Transmitted Diseases

In no other area is preparation more important than when dealing with STDs. There's frightfully little about this topic that's funny, and it may be the one area of our sexual lives that cannot be ignored. As we said before, learning to talk to your man is essential—and you need to have this conversation to protect your good-girl Catholic reputation, if for no other reason. True, having the conversation means you're serious about the sinful act, but contracting a virus means you have gone down that road.

And no amount of denying the deed will counteract that simple fact.

It's never easy to broach this subject. It's also never easy to resist your lover when you find yourself in any of the following predicaments: in bed, half-naked, tipsy, aroused. Clearly these are the last chances you have to get the discussion going about the Clap, but truly they're the worst times. So, tip number one: Have the conversation out of the bedroom, totally clothed, dead sober and feeling fat. (Maybe broach it when you're having your period.)

Ask how he feels about getting tested. Though it seems unsexy, in truth you'll be letting him know that you're ready to at least start thinking about sex. And *that* is sexy to any guy. Remember, he'll likely tell you that he's clean, that "you have nothing to worry about, baby." Whatever the man in your life says, you need to first evaluate how much you trust him. And more, *why* you trust him. Do you trust him because you really, really want to? Because you're horny? Or do you trust him because he has earned it? Because you *actually* know each other. In short, because you have seen the negative test results from a doctor and lab of your choice.

> "Given a choice between hearing my daughter say, 'I'm pregnant' or 'I used a condom,' most mothers would get up in the middle of the night and buy them herself."
>
> —Jocelyn Elders

WordPlay

D-date

1. Prophylactic expiration month and year.

2. The most important piece of information printed on a condom package. (The second most important is the warning that condoms are not 100 percent effective.)

Pray It Isn't So

Let's imagine for a second that you actually decide to use the rhythm method as your preferred form of birth control. Perhaps you're feeling particularly pious. You've created a laminated, wallet-sized calendar of your rhythmic cycles.

We're not here to encourage this kind of strict behavior but, for heaven's sake, we believe that if you're going to use the Church's favorite form of birth control, you should follow it up with the practicing Catholic's second favorite: prayer. That's right. Some quick research shows that there is a saint for pretty much every need. Below we've created a handy chart to make the most of your devotions. (By the way, it's Saint Zita for lost keys.)

Friday night:

You and the girls are getting ready for a big party. Admit it, you're hoping to get lucky. Start the night off right, and say a prayer to the saint watching over you: Saint Maria Goretti (teenage girls), Saint Gabriel Possenti (college students) or Saint Matthias (plain old alcoholics).

Later that night:

You're feeling a bit sassy and more than a bit saucy. Before it's too late, say a prayer that the booze you're drinking is infused with some sort of natural birth control. Make your plea to Saint Vincent of Saragossa (wine makers), Saint Boniface of Mainz or Saint Arnulf of Soissons (brewers).

Even later that night:

You've cornered him. You're getting hot and heavy. Your final words? Say a prayer to Saint Camillus of Lellis (compulsive gambling).

Saturday morning:

The deed is done. You've placed your faith in the heavens. You're hoping your prayers paid off. You say a little post-coitus quickie to Saint Claud (bad luck).

Following Friday:

It's been a week. While watching Britney Spears shake a tail feather, you are reminded of the time in dance class when you were told you had no rhythm. You begin to doubt your ability to read your own body (or a calendar, for that matter). Offer some words up to Saint Eustace, invoked against family troubles.

Three weeks later:

You're not feeling so well. You're hoping it was the kung pao chicken. What to do? Spend some thoughtful moments with Timothy and Emerentiana, patron saints of stomachaches. Try something along these lines: "Saints Timothy and Emerentiana, up in heaven, please help ensure that the morning sickness and aversion to poultry is part of God's overall plan for me to have bellyaches and not anything more life-changing."

Just to be safe, you also may want to offer one up to Saint Cadoc, who is invoked against cramps. Only, in this case, ask him to bring the menstrual ills on.

Four to six weeks later:

Still no red flag. You're feeling the pressure big-time. You're hoping you miscalculated your cycle; you were never good at math, anyway. You're in for some serious prayer, and you need to call in the big guns: Saint Rita of Cascia (desperate cases) and Saint Jude (lost causes).

Four to five months later:

You're starting to show. There's no denying it. God has blessed you with child! Better start the cycle of life off right and start offering prayers to each of the following:

Saint Raymond Nonnatus (obstetricians)
Saints Gangulphus and John-Francis Regis (happy marriage)
Saint Gomer (unhappy husbands)
Saints Gerard Majella and Margaret (childbirth) and
Saint John of Bridlington (complications in childbirth)
Saint Brigid of Ireland (newborns)
Saint Martina (nursing mothers)
Saint Concordia (babysitters)

Roving Reporter

Do you suppose it's a coincidence that your friendly family pharmacist looks all saintly in a white lab coat and stands on a platform two feet above ground level peering down? We asked our panel: "How did you first get contraception?"

Vincent Kelly, 50
Married with ten kids

"Contraception? Buddy, I got ten kids."

Jimmy McCracken, 15
Fordham Prep sophomore

"We didn't need it. We used a fizzy drink to stop her from getting pregnant."

Danny and Francesca Gallo, both 29
Newlyweds

> Francesca answers for both:
> "Our parents."
> (In truth, Danny stole some expired condoms
> from his dad's dresser, and Francesca went on the
> Pill in high school to "regulate her periods.")

Iris Sullivan, 65
Unmarried

> "I once got a flavored variety pack from a Secret
> Santa. Tossed it. But if I knew then what I know
> now, I would have used them and used them
> some more."

Andrea Perez, 22
Recent college grad

> "Me? Please, my guys come prepared or they
> don't come at all."

"I want to tell you a terrific story about oral contraception. I asked this
girl to sleep with me, and she said 'no.' "

—Woody Allen

Chapter Four

The Aftermath

Counting your blessings:
How to deal with it and do it again.

It's a Done Deed

Lost but not forgotten

So it's official—you're not a virgin anymore. What's next? A lot.

Most girls we spoke with reported waking up the morning after their first time with two equally intense but conflicting feelings: "Whoo-hoo! I did it! He loves me." And, "Omigod, what have I done?" Many, in fact, told tales of tackling this conflict immediately after the deed and being none-too-shy about expressing their remorse to a glowing partner. Big mistake. Be like his condom and act ultrasensitive. His ego probably can't handle your doubts.

Here are some morning-after suggestions for acting after the act. Think of them as Emily Post for Parochial Girls.

Take a Long, Hot Bath

Wash your guilt away. The idea is an oldie but a goodie. As you cleanse your body, you literally can feel your soul shine. Take a hint from your shampoo bottle—rinse and repeat. Note: It may take several attempts for this little act to take effect, but just remember that cleanliness is next to godliness.

Think Before You Speak

This is a good rule of etiquette no matter how you cut it, but it's especially pertinent here. Are you really sure you're ready to divulge your night's dalliances with your girlfriends? Instead, start by spilling it to your diary. Then wait a while. Next go to a place where you can be assured of your privacy and quietly tell an imaginary friend. When you really can't keep your mouth shut any longer, choose one trusted friend (not several) and let her know.

Let Him Call You

Hey, listen, we're cool chicks. Seriously. We don't follow rigid and traditional courtship rules—that's not our book. We don't play games. We've even been known to make the first move. However, this is one situation that merits a bit of coyness. If he's the right guy, he should know to call you, he should know to bring you flowers and he should know to be there for you. You've just given him a precious gift. It's his turn to pony up.

Avoid Your Folks

Suddenly have *a lot* of work to do that day (frequent showering is chore number one). The less eye contact with mom and dad, the better. Remember, you will feel OK again, but the day after might leave you just a little too freaked out to have a chat with the 'rents.

Steer Clear of Church

Same concept as the mom-and-dad factor. The best plan would be to lose your virginity on a weeknight so you have a few days to get used to your new status. But if, like so many girls, your big night is a Saturday, feign a sore throat (invoke Saint Blaise to help you out), and stay safely ensconced in front of the TV.

A couple of Catholic gals said they deliberated having sex for so long that, by the time it happened, sex was a walk in the pure-of-heart park. When you know the time is right, how can anything feel wrong? Listen to Lucy: "The next day, my guy and I were walking hand-in-hand down the street. He turned and asked me, 'How do you feel now that you've finally lost it?' 'Lost it?' I said. 'I don't think I lost anything. . . . I've gained everything!'" Wouldn't it be nice—albeit non-Catholic—if we all felt that way?

Bible Pop Quiz

Soon after Adam and Eve ate the forbidden fruit, they:
   a.   Felt full.
   b.   Took a sip of wine.
   c.   Had a nap.
   d.   Felt shame and realized they were naked.

Answer: d

Papa Don't Preach

He looks at you funny. Yes, you're certain. Your dad knows. How does he know? He just does. Still uncertain? Take this quiz to find out how much he knows:

1. At dinner, you ask your father to pass the potatoes. He:
   a. Grunts.
   b. Passes them but does not lift his eyes from the pool of gravy on his plate.
   c. Hands them to you and asks if you will be needing the butter as well.

2. You want to borrow the car for the night. You begrudgingly ask dad. His reply:
   a. Unquestionable silence.
   b. "No."
   c. "Of course. Just remember to fill 'er up!"

3. Your father is sitting outside, reading the latest John Grisham thriller. You approach him cheerfully and ask how the book is. He:
   a. Nervously cleans off his reading glasses.
   b. Monotonously explains, "Just like the rest."
   c. Details the characters, the climax and the denouement, then poses a question about the underlying meaning of it all.

4. You come home from school with your latest report card—all As except for an uncharacteristic C+ in calculus. When you show your father your grades, he:

    a. Signs his name in silence.

    b. Looks at you disapprovingly and mutters, "A C+, huh? You must have turned your books in for boys."

    c. Says, "Good job, hon. An A for effort."

5. Your parents return from vacation, having left you home alone. With a clean house and a convincing smile, you ask how their trip was. Your father:

    a. Starts unpacking, tools around in the garage and changes a lightbulb,

    b. Hands you a Vatican snow globe and does a complete home search for contraband.

    c. Brings you back Rome's best (read: shoes) and emphasizes how much he missed you.

If you answered mostly as and bs:

He knows. There is nothing you can do. Avoid all interaction until he comes to terms with it.

If you answered mostly cs:

He knows deep down. He's just in denial.

Roving Reporter

Secrets are lies, and bad manners besides. "Who did you spill the beans to first after you lost your virginity?"

Vincent Kelly, 50
Married with ten kids

> "Well, it was pretty apparent at the altar, what with Diane six months' pregnant and all."

Jimmy McCracken, 15
Fordham Prep sophomore

> "Anyone who would listen."

Danny and Francesca Gallo, both 29
Newlyweds

> Francesca answers for both:
> "Like all other young men, he told his best buddies. I didn't tell anyone right away because I thought it should be shared just with that special someone. Eventually my best girlfriend got it out of me, though."
> (In truth, Danny had lied to his buddies years earlier about losing it, and Francesca called her friend the second it was over to giggle about how bad it was.)

Iris Sullivan, 65
Unmarried

> "The beans are still canned. But if I knew then what I know now, I would have shouted it and shouted it some more."

Andrea Perez, 22
Recent college grad

> "I called Anna and Allison simultaneously on three-way, and then Allison got call-waiting, so she told Emily . . ."

> "It is now quite lawful for a Catholic woman to avoid pregnancy by a resort to mathematics, though she is still forbidden to resort to physics and chemistry."
>
> —H. L. Mencken

WordPlay

Shagging
British sex.

Whoopie
The Newlywed Game sex.

Your First Scare

Testing your anxiety

It may have happened to you within moments of losing your virginity. Hey, it may even have happened to you within moments of first rounding third base. If not, it's bound to happen to every Catholic girl at some (or, for most, several) moments during your premarital sex life: You think you're pregnant.

You recalculate your cycle. You read the back of a condom package and find out that rubbers aren't 100 percent effective. You remember the stories of your friend's older sister who was *on the Pill* and still got pregnant. Dwelling on it, you think, is probably making the pregnancy stick. Now you agonize, because you know there is a fate worse than being a single mom: undeniable evidence that you have actually had sex. Your parents and teachers will know.

The first thing you do is figure out how you can convince those around you—namely your mom, dad and family priest—that you have in fact become the bearer of the Second Coming. You pore over religious texts to begin your tale of an annunciation, the Holy Spirit and a feeling you can only describe as God within you.

"Scrap that," you think. "Miracles like that can really only happen once." So you call your friends. You discuss the predicament. Luckily, your best friend is wiser than you. Your hysterical tears subside a bit, and she asks you the practical stuff: "Did you use protection?"

"Yes, we used a condom and I'm on the Pill."

"OK," she says, "When was the middle of your cycle?"

"Two and a half weeks ago."

"OK," she says. "Call me when you have a real problem." She hangs up.

The next day, you get your period and have never been happier to welcome the womanly mess. Until the next time . . .

"Flee fornication."

—1 Corinthians 6:18

WordPlay

Pregnancy test

1. The scariest and longest seven minutes of one's life, during which one debates one's entire existence, beliefs and morals.

2. An exam no Catholic girl can prepare for, no matter how many all-nighters are pulled.

What a Nightmare!

Twenty-eight-year-old Alyssa describes her recurring experience with a phenomenon all too familiar to us modern Catholic girls:

"For me, sex came with bad dreams. The basic plot was always the same: I was pregnant and I was single. My parents, aunts, grandmother and family priest were just about to find out. There were some variations: I would be pregnant with twins, a double-duty dirty deed. Or my boyfriend fled without a trace—they weren't even his children. I woke up in a panic each morning, clutching my belly. I would eventually calm down and happily begin my day knowing it had all been a very bad dream.

"The nightmares continued through all three of my sexual relationships. They were at their worst with Dan, a hot, would-be video artist I dated post-college. He didn't believe people who loved each other needed labels. In short, he ran from commitment. So my anxiety during my four-month fling with Dan escalated to terror-filled dreams that involved revealing my premarital pregnancy and explaining the nonboyfriend status—big gasp—of the father.

"All of this might sound easy enough to relate to. All single women have some I-can't-be-pregnant stress, right? Right. Oh, but my neurosis was far more developed than most. For one, I had been on the Pill since three weeks after my first sexual encounter AND I always made my partner wear a condom. Plus, I almost never had sex during days 13, 14, 15 of my cycle. If my period was more than four hours late, I took a pregnancy test. I've peed on enough sticks to warrant some sort of merit badge. I can't wait for my wedding night, so I can finally get some sleep."

Having Sex Again

Because your first time won't be your last time

By some divine miracle, you get through the emotional turmoil of your first time. You may have even had a positive experience. Now comes doing it again. There are two ways to go back to the sexual well. One is with the first guy. The second is with Mr. New Guy. Eventually you'll do it again and again and again. If you're lucky, you may even enjoy it. Here's how.

You've seen pictures in books. You've heard tales from your non-Catholic girlfriends. You may even have imagined some new ones yourself. That's right, we're talking about different positions. The weekly forty-five-minute Church calisthenics—kneeling, standing, sitting, up and down, up and down, up and down—you endured as a girl will finally pay off. It might be less holy, but this workout is a lot more fun.

Below you'll find the straight talk. Every other position we've heard of is a variation on one of these. We left out the really kinky stuff. For that kind of lesson, you'll need to get your mind into a more pornographic publication, dirty girl!

WordPlay

Impregdate

Many Catholic couples' engagement day.

The Missionary

This is the standard, first-time position. It's the standard, period. It could be called the Original Sin.

What you may not know: The term came from actual missionaries preaching the sanctity of the position to natives in the South Pacific.

Tip: Though morally sound, in some sense it might not always be the most exciting for you. Try getting him to, plainly, ride you a little higher. Pelvic bone + clitoris = Oh my God!

Woman on Top

We actually knew a girl who called this the Proud Mary. Call it what you like, this is the second standard in your sexual oeuvre.

What you may not know: Although you may feel grossly inadequate and insecure the first time (or first few times) you attempt this empowering position, the truth is that most men (and definitely the worthwhile ones) welcome this kind of initiative in their lady.

Tip: Turn yourself around and face the other way. The visual your man gets is best after a few fanny reps at the gym.

Doggie Style

You're kneeling beside your bed saying your nightly prayers when you drop your Rosary beads. You get on all fours and begin to search around for your mother-of-pearl special baubles your grandma gave you at your Confirmation. Freeze frame: Take this bowed-down position onto the bed the next time you're with your man. For you novices, this does NOT mean anal sex in any way, shape or form. It simply means the man enters the woman from behind.

What you may not know: The lack of eye contact stops sin from staring you in the face. Plus this position leaves the man's hands free to touch your front parts, which makes it WOW!

Tip: If your knees start to buckle, try this position lying down. You also can give it a try by standing up and bending over your kitchen table or your bed or other furniture. This would be called the crazy-dog-on-hind-legs style.

Standing Up

Think of this as Giving Each Other the Homily. In general, there's no dominant partner in this position. Standing, you're both equals. And equal control means equal pleasure (we hope).

What you may not know: Height matters (enough said).

Tips: 1. Find a ledge for your foot—a soap dish, a bedside table, whatever. 2. If you're up against a door, beware of the knob.

Sitting

More fun than parking your rear on Saint Elizabeth's hard oak pew or the three-decades-old desks at Saint Lucy's, this position can take two forms: straddling your seated man or making yourself cozy in his lap.

What you may not know: Whether your low-budget kitchen chairs can handle the weight. Test them out in advance.

Tip: Even though you're on top, your tootsies might not reach the floor, making it more difficult for you to control your movements. Let him shoulder some of the work from beneath. See if all the squats he did on the football field really paid off.

Destination Everywhere

The key to fun sex is often where you do it. Just like real estate, it's all about location, location, location. And suggestions abound. We surveyed loads of women and men about their favorite erotic environments. We left out the most common responses—airplanes, libraries and kitchen tables—and opted for the more exotic locales. Here are the top five:

1. Italy: The boot repeatedly came out on top. Hmm, a country home to both fervent sexual desires and the Holy See itself?

2. Museums: We're talking big time, the Louvre, the Hermitage, Holy Land USA.

3. Ski resorts: Sounds innocent enough until you consider a snowmobile or a gondola lift. Talk about après-ski done right!

4. Stadiums: Men all over seek to score in the arena of a favorite sports team.

5. Movie theater: We reluctantly include this because, frankly, we hate seat-kickers, and sex in the balcony seems to demand it.

Big tip: If you want to learn your man's secret fantasy location, choose your words wisely. Most guys answer the question "Where would you most like to have sex?" with "In the butt."

WordPlay

Meat

1. Something Catholics can't eat on Fridays during Lent.

2. Hot freshmen.

3. Male privates.

Love, Italian Style

Sexperienced Professionals

Getting outside advice

You've had good sex, but you want fantastic sex. Your man leaves you satisfied but not exactly coming back for more. You've traded secrets with the girls, pored over your favorite women's mags and learned tricks from gay men. It's time to bring in the big guns; it's time for a professional. Sex therapists and sex-shop salesgirls can come in handy. If you're inclined to explore some nonfamilial, non-Catholic sex sources for advice on everything from how to kink it up right to giving yourself a better rubbing, here are some tips for beating the embarrassment when gabbing with a pro:

1. There are no stupid questions.
2. They've heard it all and much worse before.
3. Get on the horn. It's easier than face-to-face.
4. Remember, you run the show. Feel free to talk the talk.

"When the sun comes up, I have morals again."
—Elizabeth Taylor

Special Delivery: Writing the Perfect Dear John Letter

Your high-school sweetheart will always retain an unchallenged place in your heart as First Love. But let's face it, there comes a time in your life (read: college) when you're ready for more—more attention, more maturity, more muscle. You may feel extreme guilt in leaving your first honey—the person you lost your virginity to and the person who, in the back of your Catholic mind, you rationalized you were going to marry.

Our younger readers may not agree: "My guy is it," you may

say. "Our relationship is stronger than distant campuses." Trust us, once you're immersed in collegiate life, the majority of young bonds quickly whither and die. Expect a shelf life of one semester. You'll be free by Christmas break your freshman year. Not to worry. There are dorms full of young men hoping to take his position. Or, at least, take up position with you. We've taken the guesswork out of how to make a successful—but not too painful—cut with your high-school love. When the time comes to get over your get-away-from-me guilt, you'll want to be prepared with the right tools. Use our suggestions below. (For you twenty- and thirtysomethings, these epistles can also be adapted for your post-college breakups. Think email, corporate memo, voice mail.)

First Love, Still in Love

He's sweet, he's affectionate. He is still very much in love with you despite the distance and open relationship you've imposed.

Tip: This is not a guy you just throw away. You need carefully crafted language to help preserve the right to revisit your relationship during long weekends at home and the ever-important summer break, while still ensuring your guilt-free romps with the captain of the lacrosse team. Try incorporating some or all of the following words and phrases:

- This is the hardest letter I've ever had to write.
- I will always love you.
- It's so hard for me to be this far away from you.
- I miss you so much every day and just think it's time we grew on our own a little bit.
- . . . back together someday.
- I feel like I'm holding you back.
- I am very much aware that this may be the biggest mistake of my life.

The Guy with Similar Doubts

His lag time between phone calls grows longer and longer. You haven't heard an unsolicited "I love you" in weeks. He didn't even make it home on the last mini-break weekend.

Tip: Do it before he does. That way, he won't have any of the "I broke her heart" guilt, which might severely hurt your chances of saving him for a rainy day. Plus, if delivered correctly (aim for confidence, style, self-assuredness), he just might change his tune and be begging for more by Easter weekend—just about the time you'll want to renew your romance, if only for a night. Craft your message with these carefully selected words:

- Hey, you [says I'm breezy and easygoing, no psychos here].
- I don't think it says anything about us if we take a break for a bit.
- I want to make sure that we are both doing the right thing.
- Being best friends could be really great.
- No pressure.

The "I Can't Believe I Ever Even Dated This Guy" Guy

This is the guy whom you now look back on not so fondly as an error in judgment, an attraction that went awry: He's a quiet conservative; you're a screaming liberal. He's bored in museums; you're a culture vulture. He believes in the death penalty; you're about ready to sentence him. He's probably a perfect match—just not for you. Here's the thing to keep in mind with this guy: You can be honest, quick and to the point, because you're not desperately concerned about his potentially broken heart. Sure, you care, but not *that* much. And as far as recycling this one . . . well, you'll worry about that later—much later. Try these lines on for size:

- I think it's time we went our separate ways.

- I think if you look carefully at our relationship, you'll see, as I do, that we really don't have much in common.
- I hope your freshman year is kick-ass.
- Call me if you need anything [you're not entirely abandoning him].

The "What a Jerk" Guy

Your oh-so-hot boyfriend has turned out to be an oh-so-not good guy. A girl has answered your late-night phone calls to his room more than once. Last you loved, you are pretty sure he called you Amy or Alex or some such. You find out his wandering eye didn't start after he went off to college. He's been scamming on you since you first agreed to be a couple back in junior year of high school. Of course, we Catholics preach forgiveness. And you should forgive him. Later. Today, destroy him. Here's a sample letter you can use to garner revenge.

> You disgusting excuse for a human being: I can't believe I wasted so many fake orgasms on you.
>
> Regretfully,
>
> _____

P.S.: Losing your hard-on IS a big deal, and it DOESN'T happen to everyone.

Chapter Five

The Math

Catholic number-crunching: When NOT having sex is the key

> *"Self-denial is the shining sore on the leprous body of Christianity."*
>
> —OSCAR WILDE

"How many people have you had sex with?" a new suitor asks. Ugh. He did it. He asked the question. The age-old quantitative query that makes every Catholic girl first blush, second sigh, and third think. The inquiry has to be answered honestly, yes, but correctly. "Zero" is too scary—there's too much on the line. "Ten" reaches double digits and borders on sluttiness. "Five" is respectable. Yeah, five is good, five is alive.

How can a sexually vibrant, young Catholic woman maintain this middle ground? The answer is simple: Catholic arithmetic. Read on for the *new* new math.

The Move
(a.k.a. The Catholic Girl's Pelvic Shift)

The ins and outs (and outs and ins)
of stepping up to the line but not crossing
over it

"The Move," that's what we call it. It's when Catholic girls don't *actually* have sex. It's the ultimate battle, the tumultuous rise and fall of Catholic guilt. The name was coined one night with a couple of girlfriends, all who happened to be Catholic. Our friend Maria had been on a date the previous night. Like all gaggles of girls, we wanted details. We dug right in: "Did you have sex last night?"

"Well, not really," she said sheepishly.

"What do you mean?" we asked back. And then she explained: She described something that was so close to home—a situation that rings true to most Catholic girls. She described the Catholic Girl's Pelvic Shift.

You know the drill. You're with a guy, messing around. Things are getting hot and heavy, and he tries to take things a little further. You are very aroused; you are having fun. He slips it in. Happy for a second, you accept this entrance into the sacred land. But then, oh wait! You can't do this! You wriggle free. Nothing is said. More kisses, petting. He's working it again. You feel comfortable. You want it. He goes in for the kill. Happy, happy . . . then, "oh no," you think, "I can't be having sex with this person." You slide sneakily out. He's amazed at your dexterous maneuvering. He doesn't know that you've been trained in ultimate sex avoidance. It could have been a lesson in gym class—working the hips to come undone. Alas, the constant struggle persists. In (oh yes), out (thank heavens). The internal forces are battling for control: guilt on one side and guilty pleasure on the other.

He finally says, "God, you are the hardest person to have sex with!"

You smile and say, "I'm Catholic, what do you expect? And for the record, we are NOT having sex." It's The Move, that's all. The Catholic girl's trick to *not* having sex—yet another piece in the premarital puzzle.

The Move

You've read about it. You've thought about it. Maybe you've even done it. Here it is, the illustrated guide to doing The Move in three easy steps.

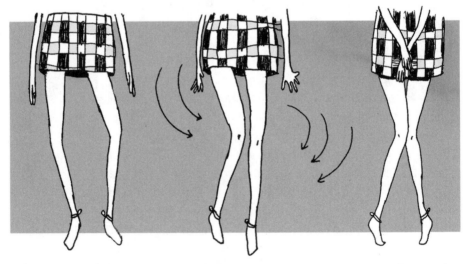

Step 1. You're lying back, accepting your lover's advances. He enters slightly. You allow the hesitant entrance. Until . . .

Step 2. You swivel your hips in a clockwise motion (lefties might try counterclockwise) and wriggle free his manhood.

Step 3. You're free. Look longingly at your lover and make it clear that things are going a little faster than you like. Until . . .
Repeat Steps 1–3.

The Quick Shot (a.k.a. The Boy's Pelvic Thrust)

But there's more to it. There are variations—something we can't peg just on Catholic girls, because it is unfortunately more widespread. This time, *he's* the one who calls it quits, and religion has nothing to do with it. You know him: He's the Quick Shot. He's got no staying power, no stamina. And when there aren't enough thrusts in the day, it isn't sex to us Catholic girls. In and out and *out*!? That's just testing the waters, and even though he's flowing, you're on the shore. Safe and sound. Another sexual situation solved. You still haven't done the deed, officially.

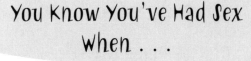

You Know You've Had Sex When . . .

So at what point can you admit you've done the nasty? Relax, we have a tip sheet.

1. You're pregnant.

2. Your anxiety is so overwhelming that it must have been sex.

3. You can't look your father in the eye.

4. There are witnesses. (Get your mind out of the gutter. His grandmother walked in on you.)

5. He calls you his girlfriend, so it's a legit "relationship." He counts!

Bible Pop Quiz

Noah's son Ham was cursed for what?

a. Glimpsing his father naked and covering him up.
b. Lusting after pork products.
c. Having sexual relations with his half-sister.
d. Murdering his mother.

Answer: a

"I like to have a martini,
Two at the very most.
After three I'm under the table,
After four I'm under my host!"

—Dorothy Parker

Reduce, Reuse, Recycle

Why sleeping with an ex doesn't count

So you've mastered The Move, and now you're ready for an accelerated lesson in keeping the numbers down: recycling the former flame. The ex is essential to Catholic math, because, quite simply, once you've broken him in, there's plenty of going back. You can satisfy your libido *and* maintain your saintly number: You've been there, done that. It's guiltless sex. We like to think we're saving the environment—our sexual environment. We reduce, reuse and recycle. We keep our numbers low.

Ironically, guys like to brag about getting their exes back in the sack. "I sleep with exes because they're so easy," he may claim. Poor fool. Little does he know that *he's* the one being used by a modern Catholic girl. He's not a new partner. Ex-sex doesn't count.

Luring the lapsed lover may seem like an arduous task. But unless there are some fragments of a broken heart left (which makes the rekindling easier though morally hard hard hard), it's a simple feat. It's all about finesse.

Drunken Dialies

Late night guarantees a quick and easy booty call. No strings, no small talk. Just sex sex sex. A simple phone call (normally done with a couple of Sidecars in you) can reap great benefits. Just remember to incorporate these three phrases: "I'm drunk," "I miss you" and "I'm horny." Straightforward yet illicit. He should be over in less than twenty minutes.

Cup of Joe

Afternoon coffee is a bit more involved (an after-work drink is a sure thing). You want to catch up. See what's new in his life. Rehash four (at the very least) great times shared. Look longingly in his eyes. Perhaps shed a tear thinking about your former relationship. If he's ready to be recycled, he'll give you a consoling hug. You kiss his neck. Whisper, "I really miss you, _____." Ask if you can talk more at your place because you don't want to get emotional in public. Enough said: You're sexually satisfied (for now) without having to carve a new notch in your bedpost.

On the Town

A night out with your ex and a group of friends requires some serious signaling. You all go out and have a blast. It's fun fun fun. But how will he know you want him again? Longing looks (see Cup of Joe) are key. Maybe a shy smirk. Offer to buy him a drink. Steal away for a quick gossip about Julia and Tom. Share an inside joke. As the night begins to wind down, inform your girlfriends of your plan. They are essential to a suave and smart exit with the ex. The others all want to go home; you don't want to go anywhere. Ask him to stay with you for "one more drink." Once alone, firmly grasp his knee as you laugh at *everything* he says. Gracefully brush his shoulder on the way to the ladies room. Playful petting is a must. There's no turning back. He'll be in the cab with you before the ice in his drink melts.

> "Self-denial is not a virtue: it is only the effect of prudence on rascality."
>
> —George Bernard Shaw

In a Constant State

Other tricks to keep your numbers low

So, we've got The Move. We recycle our exes. Catholic girls certainly know the key to fuzzy math. But there's more. Besides the obvious mental maneuver—repeating twenty times over, "It didn't happen"—a Catholic girl can swirl and twirl in a constant state of denial with these little-known devices:

Keep Your Mouth Closed

"Silence is golden," reads an intuitive proverb. This is the ultimate trick to erasing the escapade.

- Never talk to him about it. Better yet, never talk to him again.
- Never admit the act to anyone—your sister, your best friend, your dog. Remember this brainteaser? *If a tree falls in a forest but no one is around to hear it, did the tree really fall?* Well, translated to Catho-lingo, if a woman has sex but no one hears about it, did she have sex? The answer is a resounding no.
- Never admit the act to yourself. This means no journal entries. Push out and block all memories of the matter. You should not give it a moment's thought, because what's there to think about? It never happened.

Church Chat

On the flip side of the silent game is a basic practice of Catholicism: penance and absolution. When you feel the need to erase a bit of your tally, head to confession to admit all your new partners since your last penance. Confess that you've had premarital sex with two (new) men. After reciting the Act of Contrition, your priest will send you on your way, forgiven and therefore absolved of another number. This is nice and neat: Confessing two partners negates one. Admitting relations with four negates two. See how it works? And all with the Church's blessing. Lest you think you'll work your way back to your virginal ways, be warned: Absolution can halve your numbers, sure, but it can't erase them entirely. Refer to the penance chart in chapter two for more sacramental solutions.

Dionysian Denial

"I was drunk," you say, "really drunk." Guess what? Complete vindication. You weren't of sane mind. The red wine made you a bit saucy. A bit frisky. You can't even remember if it happened. Did it happen? Doubtful.

Statute of Limitations

Ten years later, can you even remember his name? (Yes, of course you can, but we don't need to know that.) There is a sexpiration date on all past partners. The scale is for you to decide. The standard is ten years—a decade anew. Extra credit: If it was "just that once," then knock it down to five years. Once doesn't *really* count, anyway, does it?

Denominational Doubt

He isn't even Catholic. That's all there is to it. He simply isn't Catholic, so how could it count? This *is* starting to sound desperate, we know, but think of it like this: If the Church doesn't recognize marriage with him, why does the rest of it take on such weighty significance? And, there's more: If he is Catholic, is he Catholic *enough*? Take the quiz in this chapter to find out.

Naughty Breaks

Vacations don't count—a cardinal rule when dealing with denial. People love saying, "Screw it, I'm on vacation," when overindulging in dessert, wine, shoe shopping . . . well, you get the point. Catholic girls take it one step further. The Australian you met at the hostel in Cinque Terre? He doesn't count. The San Franciscan stoner who showed you where Jack Kerouac used to hang? He doesn't count, either. Now don't go thinking that Catholic girls are backpacking for babes. It's just that, while on our guilt-free getaways, there's a different set of standards.

Phone-y Philandering

The phone rings in the middle of the night. It's your current guy stuck in Fresno, calling collect, and he's lonely. He wants to talk. But he doesn't just want to talk. He wants to *talk*. He's in a phone booth whispering lewd plot lines. Forty-five minutes later, you two have had quite a night. Or have you? The power of suggestion, even accompanied by secretion, does not equate. The only numbers we find here are the dollars (gasp) on your next phone bill.

Butt No!

Dramatic side note: We would be remiss if we didn't mention one more denial tactic we hear rumors of. Brace yourself. Lots of good girls supposedly use anal sex to maintain their virginity and (later) their low numbers. Gross.

"I have not had sex in almost two years, and I think once you hit two years, you automatically get your virginity back."
—Margaret Cho

WordPlay

Sexpiration date

In Catholic math, the date a sexual encounter is no longer counted.

Top Methods of Denial

Cut out this cheat sheet and keep it handy for the next time you find yourself in a moral bind asking, "Did I or didn't I?" You most certainly did NOT if:

1. It was just for a second.
2. It was over the phone.
3. He was an ex.
4. You've never told a soul.
5. You've never spoken with him again.
6. You received absolution from your priest.
7. You were drunk, REALLY drunk.
8. You were on vacation.
9. It was forever ago.
10. It was just once.
11. He's an atheist.
12. It was bad, REALLY bad.

Is He Catholic Enough to Count?

So you've done the deed—maybe—and want to know if he's worthy of an admission. He's a Catholic, so there's a good chance he counts. Or is there? Ask yourself these five simple questions. If you answer yes to three or more, then sorry, sister—he counts. However, if you answer no to three or more, it never happened (well, sort of).

1. Does he remember his Confirmation name? (Bonus: If he doesn't even know what a Confirmation name is, then pass Go—you're safe. He's not a *real* Catholic.)
2. Does he attend church regularly, as on Sundays?
3. Does he know which number Pope John Paul we're up to?
4. Can he tell you when Vatican II occurred?
5. Can he recite the Beatitudes?

Charlotte: How can you forget a guy you've slept with?

Carrie: Toto, I don't think we're in single digits anymore.

—*Sex and the City*

Inverse Proportions

Comprehending the world of Catholic boys' math

You think we Catholic girls failed sophomore-year Logic 101? Try treading the often more complicated world of a *boy's* number theorems. It's enough to make your calculator come undone. He lowers the numbers for his gal, and he ups them for his pals. You see, in the same way that we *won't* count the half-truths and near-realities or even discuss the situation with our friends for fear of losing our good-girl reputation, they *must* count the partial-facts and somewhat-accurates and also tell as many friends, fraternity brothers and strangers as possible to secure their bad-boy reputation.

Most women know, understand and have come to expect, really, some white lies from their man. He fibs and whispers sweet remarks to ensure his unchallenged place in your heart and—more importantly for him—his access (nay, his right) to your nether regions. Perhaps his white lie is just insisting, "No respectable guy *really* thinks Pamela Anderson is sexy." Maybe it's telling you that, despite the freshman (or twenty) pounds you gained, "You look HOT in your cut-up-to-there black miniskirt, baby." Oh, but it goes deeper than that.

WordPlay

Easy-bake oven

1. Popular culinary toy for the under-10 set responsible for batches of undercooked brownies and swigs of Pepto-Bismol.

2. Promiscuous girl who is always in heat.

Did She Really?

Amanda, age 28

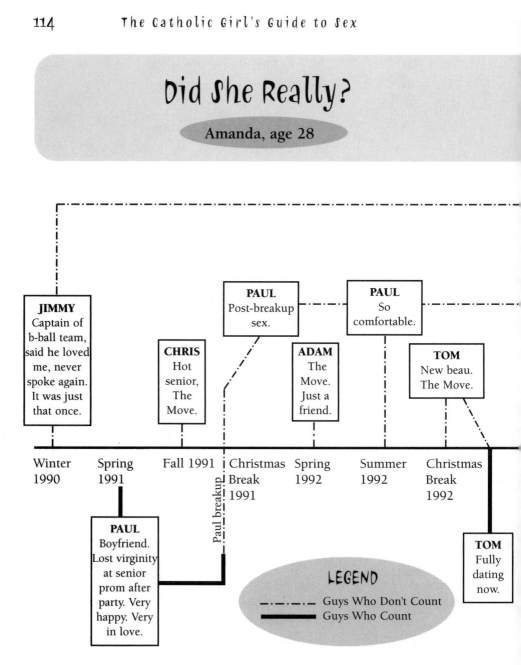

JIMMY
Captain of b-ball team, said he loved me, never spoke again. It was just that once.

CHRIS
Hot senior, The Move.

PAUL
Post-breakup sex.

ADAM
The Move. Just a friend.

PAUL
So comfortable.

TOM
New beau. The Move.

Winter 1990

Spring 1991

Fall 1991

Christmas Break 1991

Spring 1992

Summer 1992

Christmas Break 1992

Paul breakup

PAUL
Boyfriend. Lost virginity at senior prom after party. Very happy. Very in love.

TOM
Fully dating now.

LEGEND
—·—·—·— Guys Who Don't Count
———— Guys Who Count

We Catholic girls have quantitative reasoning that would make Einstein's head spin. For a sneak peek into the science of it all, check out the graph below, which charts one young woman's (non)sexual history.

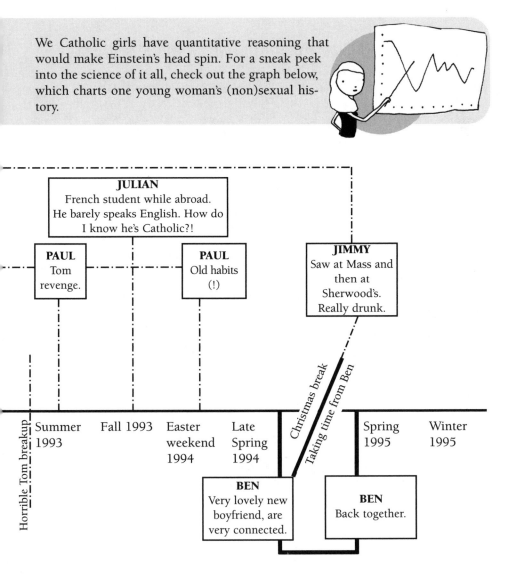

But Mom, Those Are MY Boxers!

Sometimes denying your guy(s) to your mom takes an even more complicated solution than hiding the truth from yourself. Consider our galpal Lauren's plight:

"I was raised in an Italian Catholic family, and we weren't just a Christmas and Easter family. We were full-blown Sundays. Needless to say, we had boyfriend rules.

"Guys in the bedroom? Hell, no. Guys in the bedroom, door open? With a VERY watchful eye and only under special circumstances. Guys in the basement? So long as mom can interrupt every fifteen to twenty minutes in order to offer popcorn, provide iced tea, supply brownies or cookies, get wrapping paper, empty the dehumidifier, check the thermostat. Guys in the family room, nestled between mom and dad? Yes, please. They mandated separate bedrooms until marriage—engagements do not count. The guest room could've been renamed the Hopeful Suitor Suite.

"As a 27-year-old woman, I still obeyed the moral code of my parents. Or, at least, I created an air of obedience—which, in a

Bible Pop Quiz

King Solomon had sex with how many women?

a.   400 wives, 200 concubines
b.   700 wives, 300 concubines
c.   10 wives, 400 concubines
d.   500 wives, 500 concubines

Answer: b

sense, makes it so. So when my boyfriend of two years lost the lease on his apartment, he naturally thought it was time we shacked up. You can imagine my anxiety. No Cicarelli woman lives in sin and is still welcomed at Sunday dinner. I learned to hide. I learned to deny. I learned to lie.

"Phillip was patient. He dealt with a collapsible dresser. He managed with his clothes placed underneath a covert top layer of female sweaters. Everything had to be in a neat, easily packable and portable storage system. No masculine touch. One toothbrush only. No electric razors. No sports magazines. No Phillip on the answering machine—no Phillip answering the phone. For mom's bimonthly visits, we were in the closet, literally. Anything conspicuous or Phillip-possible was stuffed in the back of the hall closet. I kept her time short. But she knew, I'm convinced. She has the nose of a Catholic, the sense for sin. But she never uttered an accusation. She just smiled and nodded.

"Dating a Catholic woman is not easy. It comes with a world of dos and don'ts. Lucky for me, Phillip put up with the don'ts. And for that I bought him a new toothbrush, but only *after* he bought me a ring."

Over cocktails one night with a group of friends, the subject of losing one's virginity came up. This absorbing topic was made all the more interesting by John's revelation to Christy, his girlfriend, that he "lost his virginity" several times. We girls listened intently while the boys smirked knowingly. "What?" Christy inquired, completely confused.

"Well, I lost my virginity for the first time with Nancy at Jason's my-parents-are-trying-to-rekindle-the-passion-in-Hawaii party," explained John. "Then, later in the summer, I was on Cape Cod and met Jen, another good Catholic girl. I knew I had a decent shot at being with her, so one night when we were hot and heavy in the dunes, I told her how I wanted to 'lose my virginity' with her, that she was 'precious' and 'the one.' Done. 'Easy enough,' I thought. And from there it went on like that with every girl—and there were a *bunch* of them.

"Until college, when it really wasn't necessary any-more. For one, I met non-Catholic girls who didn't have such hang-ups. And two, it would have been kind of pa-thetic, really. See, being a virgin made it special for girls when we were young and innocent, but later it would have just made me seem pitiful. As though by age 19 if I *didn't* have numbers to back up my libido, then I wasn't sexworthy."

Christy was appalled. She hoped his lying was left in the past with his Samantha Fox posters. She questioned every-thing he'd ever told her. When he said, "Just twelve, sweetie," was he telling the truth? When he said, "You're the only one I've ever loved," did he mean it?

In private, John laughed at her concern. "I was in high school. I wanted to get laid. And besides, you want to know the truth? It never *really* worked."

She asked, "Then why did you lie about it at the table?"

"Because there were guys there," he said matter-of-factly.

And therein lies the inverse proportion of a boy's multi-plication tables. Fearing the wrath of an older brother—and large Catholic families are full of them—teenage boys can't name names of *actual* girls they know but rather will brag about meeting this "super-hot chick who totally wanted it" on a family trip or at camp or at his cousin's house.

The lying starts out innocently enough: Sitting next to a girl in church while on vacation becomes a date. By sophomore year, he's saying he got to first or even second base with her. By junior year, as the yarn is spun, his summer escapades with that girl two years before made him the most talked-about boy at Holy Cross High School.

Luckily, if equated correctly, his y variables and your x variables should cancel each other out in the end. Here's the trick to making the problem-solving work right in your head: DENIAL + DENIAL = VINDICATION. Haven't you learned anything in this chapter? Don't discuss your histories at length. Don't question his fakery, lest you be caught in your own. Keep your numbers where you both like them—it probably works out anyway, right? RIGHT!

"The very purpose of existence is to reconcile the glowing opinion we have of ourselves with the appalling things that other people think about us."

—Quentin Crisp

WordPlay

Lent

Forty days between Ash Wednesday and Easter Sunday observed by Catholics as a season of penitence. Things to give up: junk food, chocolate, booze, cigarettes, swearing, guilt about sex.

Roving Reporter

Some people got As in artithmetic. Others failed calculus. We gave our pollsters a math pop quiz: "How many people have you had sex with?"

Vincent Kelly, 50
Married with ten kids

(Sighs) "Just my wife."

Jimmy McCracken, 15
Fordham Prep sophomore

"So far, three. Tiffany is at college. Diane is from Montreal. Pilar is this totally hot exchange student my aunt and uncle put up for the summer."

Danny and Francesca Gallo, both 29
Newlyweds

Francesca answers for both:
"He's my third, and I'm his tenth."
(In truth, Danny has had only two women, including his current bride, and we have thus far received sixteen unconfirmed reports of Francesca's romps in the hay.)

Iris Sullivan, 65
Unmarried

> "None. But if I knew then what I know now, I would have done it and done it some more."

Andrea Perez, 22
Recent college grad

> "Well, if you count Jack, then two. And I guess if you count Robert, that would make three. But really I don't count them, so just one— Luke. Oh, and definitely Peter, and I suppose maybe Brian was a thing, but I don't really think so; I mean, we were so wasted, and it just happened that once, like, five years ago."

Chapter Six

The Rest of It

The Church bazaar: Vibrators,
virgins and vixens, oh wow!

> "To err is human—but it feels divine."

> —Mae West

Now that we've covered all the big stuff—doctrine, doing it and denying it—we think it's time we sweated the small stuff. Here you'll find everything else that makes us Catholic girls amused and ashamed, blushed and befuddled. We give you a ride through the world of self-love—and myths, fantasies and porno, to boot. Read on for the lowdown on everything you were ashamed to admit you wanted to know.

Taking Matters into Your Own Hands

Your guide to good vibrations

Growing up, we thought of masturbation as something too dirty for words. In sex ed, boys learned a little about erections and a lot about the evils of self-love; we girls learned only about menstruation and Maxi Pads. By the time we realized that people could and would even want to undertake such a seemingly sordid self-service, it was naturally assumed that it was just for the guys. Good Catholic girls wouldn't purposefully venture "down there," and, well, yucky boys will be yucky boys. But such pleasure should not be denied.

Even if you haven't reached ecstasy on your own yet, you've probably explored a bit innocently enough. It likely began with some innocuous activities that left you feeling confused. The oh-so-good running water in the bathtub or the particularly exciting day horseback riding left you feeling a bit dirty. Not to mention that you woke up with a feeling of dread after an evening of funny dreams and pillow rubbing. The nightly sensations could not be described. The clitoris was still uncharted territory. Overwhelmed with guilt, you wouldn't explore further. With no clear set of instructions or peer camaraderie, we girls colonized the kingdom of chastity while the boys were granted the land of masturbation. Sound familiar? Well, here's a little secret we hope you already know: Girls can feel good about going solo, too.

Officially speaking, of course, the Church denounced masturbation way back around A.D. 300 because, it said, the ejaculation of sperm was meant for procreation, not recreation. This got us thinking: When a woman has an orgasm, she doesn't release an egg. Whoa—we think we found a loophole. Yet there it is, shouting down at us from on high— the *Catechism of the Catholic Church,* which screams that masturbation is a big no-no for guys and gals.

All right, all right, so masturbation, like everything else we've discussed so far, is a sin. But it's all relative. Given the

risks of sex—both to your health and your Catholic reputation—it just might be a risk worth taking. What we mean to
say is: Would your mom rather you spread your legs all over
town for every Tom, Dick and Harry, or would it be more acceptable for you to get yourself off alone with forefinger,
midkid and ringo?

"We know less about the sexual life of little girls than of
boys. But we need not feel ashamed of this distinction;
after all, the sexual life of adult women is a 'dark con-
tinent' for psychology."

—Sigmund Freud

"Do we want one? Good God, no! The day Freud came up
with penis envy, I think his brains had to have been out
to lunch."

—Helen Gurley Brown

Bible Pop Quiz

Absalom was punished for what?
   a. Disrespecting his parents.
   b. Engaging in sexual relations with a concubine.
   c. Having sex in public.
   d. All of the above.

Answer: d

Oh! Onan

To illustrate the evils of masturbation, the Church cites the story of Onan (Genesis 38:9–10). In a nutshell, this damned man refused to impregnate his dead brother's wife, Tamar (check her out in chapter one, Lewd Ladies of the Bible). Instead, like many future Catholics trying to practice family planning, he pulled out each time. Thus, he "spilled his seeds on the ground." For this action, God punished Onan with death. That's right, death. Impress your friends: This is where we get the word onanism, an old-fashioned term for masturbation.

Love Thyself as He Has Loved You

You may have laid the framework of your sexual self-exploration in your teens, but experiencing it fully likely came in your twenties. Or maybe you're titillated but still timid—petrified to poke around. Consider this: A Janus survey revealed that more than half of American Catholics agree that masturbation is a natural part of life and continues in marriage. Read on for all the deets.

After college, you discover yourself in more ways than one. You begin to understand your body, your wants and desires. You get to know your sex drive and really start to figure out how things work. You've faked enough orgasms to know you want to have a real one, but you might not have a man. Or maybe you have a man who doesn't quite live up to the challenge. Or maybe, just maybe, you simply want some alone time. You need a helping hand.

Many girls (even some Catholic ones) report satisfying their clitoral curiosity with their fingers. These patient ladies take the time (and it could take a *lot* of time) to buff their muffs. They are highly skilled artisans who master the moves. For most Catholic girls, however, the commitment is too much to bear. If you're lucky enough to get even a teeny bit moist, your mind already has wandered from the hot guy next door to the church across town. With too much time on your hands, you allow the guilt to take over. So you need to pick up the pace to preserve your purity (read: manual massager).

Yes, you will feel a little ashamed buying and using your first vibrator. For Pete's sake, it *is* electric. Not to mention the fact that you're using it simply to have a big O and not to gain intimacy with your lover, let alone procreate. But get this: It's so good that you won't even have a moment in the moment to think that thought. See for yourself in Hailie's testimonial later in this chapter.

How Far We've Cum

The next time you see a blind man, consider the cause of his handicap a little more carefully. According to the physicians of yesteryear, he brought it on himself. Take a peek at some other signs and symptoms of male masturbation from a bygone era:

1. Acne
2. Bad posture
3. Hard of hearing
4. Vomiting
5. Constipation
6. Penchant for cussin'

Advanced Sex as a Second Language: The Masturbation Curse

Here are some of our favorite euphemisms for his and her self-loving:

Attitude adjustment
Beating around the bush
Beating off
Beating the bishop
Beating the meat
Bending to the will of the purple warrior
Choking the chicken
Cocking the cannon/gun
Devil's handshake
Doin' the hand jive
Dome polishing
Drilling for oil
Electroshock therapy
Engine cranking
Having sex with someone you love
Hitting the clit

Holding your own
Jerking my Johnson
Jerking off
Jerking the gherkin
Making the kitty purr
Palm piloting
Playing the slots
Pulling a Han Solo
Pushing your button
Rubbing off
Shaking hands with little big man
Spanking the monkey
Wanking your crank
Whacking off

"Hey, don't knock masturbation! It's sex with someone I love."

—Woody Allen

Why Date When You Can Vibrate?

Here's how Hailie got over it and got herself off.

"I had a problem with masturbation, but I couldn't quite put my finger on it. In college, I would attempt it but to no avail. Rather than welcoming fantasies, I would think of my disapproving mother and stop. It was ingrained in my very soul that Catholic girls couldn't, wouldn't and shouldn't do it. Plus, I thought it was really, really boring. All that work, and all I got was a case of carpal tunnel syndrome.

"When I entered my single-girl-in-the-city stage of life, I finally came into my own. My peaking sexual curiosity clashed severely with the unexciting New York City male gene pool. There was the Gucci-wearing, he-can't-be-straight ad guy who seemed more concerned with having the smallest cell phone in the room than wooing a new woman. Then there was the starving artist, trying to find his way on ten dollars a week. There was another undesirable—the steak-face hockey player from college that I saw here and there but didn't like then and certainly didn't like again. And last but not least in this Wall Street–laden city, there was the I-wish-it-was-still-the-eighties coke fiend, investment-banker guy. You get the point: Finding a man to sleep with is easy, but finding one worth the sleep-over is hard. Sometimes a woman has to improvise.

"During a gimlet-ridden dinner one night, my galpals brought up the taboo topic. Valerie relentlessly praised her Rabbit, while

Jane said, flashing her fingers, 'Who needs toys when you have these bad boys?' And there it was as clear as holy water: Everybody but me was masturbating. I couldn't believe it. Shy and embarrassed, I ended the conversation with a bad segue about the cute bartender.

"I couldn't ignore my screaming libido anymore, but aren't sex shops for perverts and whores? And my mother would DIE if she knew I was even considering getting a vibrator. Or would she? I mean it IS safer sex. I wouldn't be experimenting with a new man. It would be me, myself and I—the best kind of *ménage à trois*. A month later, feeling rather empowered, I bought my first vibrator. I spotted a small, welcoming little guy that the sales lady said gave clitoral stimulation. I grabbed it and paid, quickly.

"Once I got home, I had no idea how to use it. I mean, I knew how to turn it on, but I wasn't sure how to turn ME on. I didn't talk about it with anyone. I put it in a drawer, where it sat still all day. When I finally tried it, I was definitely clumsy, but one thing became apparent: My clitoris was a launch button for orgasms. Once pressed, I took off! Who knew it would be this easy? I put the vibrator down and thought, 'What the hell have I just done?' Then my absolute amazement washed away the guilt, and I went back for more. My friend Wendy used to joke, 'Why date when you can vibrate.' And she's right.

"So while I am a sexy single Catholic girl who can't possibly find solace in casual sex, I found someone else to go home to at night. And the best part: I never fake it."

Put Your Hands Together

Masturbation may seem as foreign to you as quantum physics, but we suspect you're secretly harboring desires. Let's get over this barrier reef. Try our quiz to find out if you're ready to take matters into your own hands.

1. True or false: Your showers sometimes last forty-five minutes.

2. Finish this sentence: You feel about your clit much the same way as:
   a. A fish feels about a bicycle.
   b. Lance Armstrong feels about his bicycle.
   c. A young girl feels about her first bicycle.

3. True or false: You like to hang out in the laundry room while washing your duds.

4. How many times have you faked an orgasm?
   a. Twice, but only because I had a headache.
   b. I wouldn't even know how to fake it.
   c. At least ten times.

5. True or false: You often wake up with a smirk on your face and don't really remember why.

6. What reading material is on your nightstand?
   a. *Playboy*—for the articles.
   b. Anything by Jackie Collins.
   c. *The Wisdom of John Paul II.*

7. True or false: You are a huge advocate of the technological age.

8. Your favorite television station is:
   a. The public-access channels.
   b. The movie networks: Cinemax, Showtime, HBO.
   c. PBS.

9. True or false: You hog the air jet in the Jacuzzi.

10. You think masturbation is:
    a. Better than *Cats*.
    b. One of the seven deadly sins.
    c. Just for the boys.

Scoring:

Give yourself one point for each true answer and zero for each false. Then score as follows for the five multiple-choice questions and add them up:

Question No. 2. a: 0, b: 2, c: 1
Question No. 4. a: 2, b: 0, c: 1
Question No. 6. a: 2, b: 1, c: 0
Question No. 8. a: 1, b: 2, c: 0
Question No. 10. a: 2, b: 0, c: 1

0–5: Innocent Irene

You may not have discovered your sexual self yet, but no worries. There's no better time than the present to take your first baby steps. Separate the divine from the Divine and surprise your crush with a smooch (and enjoy it). Come back for more later.

6–10: Curious Catherine

You've gotten a sneak preview into your sexuality but can't see the big picture. It's a good start. Put on your spelunking helmet and continue the exploration. Go get yourself some toys.

11–15: Excited Emily

Eureka! You've found it. You know your way around town, and you are in tune with your body and what makes you tick. We suspect you already have a toy chest. We even think you might be a master of handicrafts. So take the time to let your fingers do the walking.

"To love oneself is the beginning of a lifelong romance."
—Oscar Wilde

Toy Story: Your Guide to Basic Vibrators

You've taken our quiz, you've finally gotten over *that* scene in *The Exorcist,* and you've decided you're ready to delve into the world of self-love, replete with plastic lips, harnessed underwear, peach-colored dildos and vibrating animal attachments. First, you need to find the right store. A place that promotes sexual education and empowerment and that's geared toward women should help make you feel more comfortable. Avoid shops that keep their goods locked behind glass. The accessibility of products lends itself to a feeling of acceptability. (Online makes it so easy. Check out our picks in Beyond the Bible.)

The first time you walk into a sex store, even a reputable shop, can be visually overwhelming. Whizzing penises, bunny ears—a whole table full of beads and balls and blow-up babes. The size alone of the various dildos is enough to make you contemplate (probably unfavorably) every partner you've ever had. Here's a look at some basic vibrators that will help you get set and go. Once you discover a magical match, you just might find yourself turning down Saturday-night dates with living, breathing guys.

The toy: Hitachi Magic Wand, about $50.

The story: This best-selling electric wand vibrator (no batteries, it plugs in) is long and lean, with a tennis-ball-style head. Similar in size and shape to typical muscle massagers, this powerful clitoral stimulator will put speed control in your hands.
The right personality: The power-hungry, take-charge gal. She'd like to see a woman become Pope.

The toy: The Smoothie, about $16.

The story: Basic and powerful, this popular, smooth, plastic battery vibrator is intended for vaginal insertion but can also be used externally. Shaped like a missile, the noise can be just as loud.
The right personality: The girl who sticks to the basics. She's a Christmas and Easter churchgoer.

The toys: The Pocket Rocket, about $26; The Water Dancer, $28.

The story: Our fave for the beginner, these cylinders of love are small and discreet. The plastic micro-massagers are quite powerful for their size. They feature only one speed and come in a waterproof model, perfect for the shower.
The right personality: The shy girl with roommates. She hides from the congregation.

The toy: The Jewel G-Spot, about $18.

The story: This jelly-rubber number features variable speeds and a curve to vibrate specifically against the G-spot. Some models come augmented with a ridge for added clitoral stimulation.
The right personality: The girl who keeps things inside. She'll never confess.

The toy: The Butterfly, about $36.

The story: Held in position by two elastic leg straps, this plastic vibrator is placed externally for hands-free fun. Strap-on vibrators come in all shapes, speeds and sizes.
The right personality: The multi-tasker. She was the girl who, in high school, headed the soup-kitchen volunteers, won class president of Our Lady of Perpetual Help, captained the basketball team, edited the yearbook, led the choir, coordinated the annual retreat and was the most popular babysitter for Miss Manfreddi's second-grade class.

The toy: The Jack Rabbit, about $80.

The story: This whoa-nelly of a vibrator features simultaneous vaginal penetration and clitoral stimulation for double duty. The plastic pearls somersault in the rotating jelly-rubber midsection like lotto balls. The animal attachment quivers rapidly in just the right place to double your pleasure.
The right personality: The girl who craves adventure. She got caught in the woods behind the boys' school. With Vinny. *And* cigarettes.

"The one thing that it seems impossible to escape from,
once the habit is formed, is masturbation."

—D. H. Lawrence

The Masturbation Game

Think you're an expert? You'll find our game fun and informative. Play it now to test your historical know-how:

1. Vibrators first appeared in women's magazines in the first two decades of the twentieth century as a:
    a. Devil repellant
    b. Home appliance
    c. Sexual massager
    d. Children's toy

2. In 1907, the first patented handheld vibrator was not battery-powered but rather worked with:
    a. Water pressure
    b. Prayer
    c. Solar power
    d. Myrrh

3. According to guru Betty Dodson, National Masturbation Month is:
    a. Held in Des Moines
    b. May
    c. A month of atonement
    d. A pick-up line

4. In the fourteenth century, Arnaldus de Villanova prescribed this to nuns suffering from hysteria:
    a. Valium
    b. Praying
    c. A dildo
    d. The court jester

5. Which of the following foods was invented, in part, to curb the "epidemic" of masturbation?
    a   Corn flakes
    b. Graham crackers
    c. Both a and b
    d. Pigs in blankets

6. In 1994, U.S. Surgeon General Joycelyn Elders was urged to resign because:
    a. She once posed for *Playboy*.
    b. She was caught with her intern.
    c. She recommended teaching children about masturbation in school sex education.
    d. She did promotion work for Ron "The Hedgehog" Jeremy.

7. The Vatican issued a sex-education guide in 1996, claiming it will help Roman Catholics:
    a. Get off
    b. Get over the guilt
    c. Feel their love
    d. Save their children from sin

Answers; 1:b, 2:a, 3:b, 4:c, 5:c, 6:c, 7:d

Fantasy Island

Letting your imagination go wild

You've found the nerve to masturbate. You've headed to the sanctity of your bedroom filled with intimidation and intrigue, horniness and helplessness. If you grab a gadget, the first few encounters with it will be so intense that you'll already be there just as you get going. But eventually you'll get used to it, and you'll need to be aroused mentally even more than physically to achieve pleasure. What you need is a good fantasy.

If you start thinking about your bounced rent check or your friend's birthday present, you could be there for hours with the sole result of electric shock. However, there are some tricks to letting your id take control. Pious thoughts only for us modern Catholic girls? Please. Think big. Real big.

Women's sexual fantasies are generally more detailed than "naked guy ooh-ooh sticking it there." They range from damsel in distress to dominatrix, from sensual mountain scenes to the backseats of taxicabs. It's normal to be a little embarrassed about your fantasies, but, despite your Catholic upbringing, there should be no shame in having them. As obscene as they may seem, there is no wrong fantasy. We've all had them, whether it is something as starstruck as kissing Benicio Del Toro (or, admit it, maybe even Angelina Jolie) or something tastier like a naked fondue party with your friends and neighbors.

Strict Catholics beware: The holiest believers denied their fantasies and were granted canonization. But they also

WordPlay

Pulling an Ellen

Realizing that you are a lesbian.

took a beating for it. Consider St. Anthony, who resisted temptation from demon visions and was pounded senseless. We'd like to be pure of heart, but we'll take orgasm over a licking any day.

The Cream Dictionary

Padre Jorges Juan "Tito" Gomez from Mexico City and Father Dominic from Chicago interpret the most popular female fantasies so you can find out what your dreams of desire say about you:

Public sex: It starts off the same every time—you exchange sly looks. You've been touching each other throughout the night. You're at the point of ultimate yearning. His eyes imprison yours, and he holds your stare. You smile and nod. He slowly pulls up your skirt and unzips his pants. You go for it, wherever you are: the park, a dark bar, a glass elevator. You're engrossed in pleasure that is increased only by the possibility of nearby strangers.

Tito and Dom: "You are feeling guilty about something and want to get caught. You need to go to confession."

Multiple partners: You are walking down steep stairs into a small bar with your boyfriend. A great DJ is on, and you want to dance, but your guy just wants to drink. So you head to the dance floor alone and start to sashay a little. An attractive woman slithers up, and you start dancing. She pushes her body against yours, coyly letting you know she wants it. You start to get tingly. You eye your boyfriend, then look longingly back to the beautiful woman. You ask if she wants to grab a drink. Instead, she leads you and your guy to her all-white lush mansion by the sea. The three of you indulge each other all night until you pass out, drenched in sweat, gasping for air, totally satisfied. Oh, and your boyfriend still loves you the most, of course.

Tito and Dom: "You are ignoring the presence of the Lord in your relationships. You need to find God."

Transportation: You are on a train, *Risky Business–*style. The sun is going down. You and your lover are sitting closely together in a high-backed seat. The train is crowded but quiet. The rumbling along the tracks gets you excited. The farther you go, the more you want him. You reach over and unzip his pants. You're both cowering in the window, you sitting on his lap and writhing in absolute excitement.

Tito and Dom: "You are running from your fears. Go to church."

Sex with a stranger: You are napping in your bed, naked, when all of a sudden a strapping young house painter is standing above you. You had completely forgotten about your appointment. The super must have let him in. You wrap the satin sheet around yourself and lead him to the small, tight bathroom. He is flustered and oh-so innocent. You show him what he needs to do and return to bed. He reappears, sweaty, and gazes deeply. You pull him into the bed and make love all afternoon.

Tito and Dom: "You are scared of commitment. You need to get married in the House of the Lord. Soon."

Celebrity crushes: You are having breakfast at the local diner, innocently reading your newspaper. Brad Pitt walks in. There are ten empty seats, but he chooses the one next to you and sits down. You smile seductively. He orders eggs over easy with a side of rye toast. Just like you. It's a code; you think, "He's enamored." He asks you for the ketchup: another double meaning, you're sure of it. You're speaking a secret language to one another. You pretend you don't know how famous he is. He likes that. He says you have a great smile. You smile even bigger. He gets up to pay for his breakfast *and* yours. He leaves his hotel room key next to your plate. He walks out and winks. You drool.

Tito and Dom: "You are superficial. You need to volunteer at a soup kitchen."

Tito and Dom's Hit List

- Bondage: "You are feeling trapped in the world. You need to pray."
- Playing the victim: "You want to be disciplined. You need to see a nun."
- Role playing: "You are uncomfortable with yourself. You need to join a convent."
- Uniform play: "You are looking for rules and guidance. You need to let Jesus into your life."
- Voyeurism: "You are curious about other cultures. You need to take a trip to the Vatican."

WordPlay

Dirtbird
Slut.

Liquid Dreams

You're stumped and need a little power of suggestion. Here are some scenes to think about over and over and over again:

1. Recall your most exciting sexual experience. Get all the juicy details right in your head. Now make the leading

man Jimmy Fallon. Pretend he's taking you to the
Saturday Night Live after-party.
2. Think of your favorite game: Chinese checkers, canasta,
    Parcheesi. Now, in your mind, invite hot people to your
    game night and change the rules. Make it a strip version.
3. Imagine you are on a cruise of the Greek islands. The
    crew is at your beck and call. You ring a bell for an oil
    massage, and a hot young lad is on hand for pampering
    and pulsating.

"The difference between pornography and erotica is
lighting."

—Gloria Leonard

Bare in Mind

Here's a sneak peek into the mundane sexual fantasies of our
male counterparts:

1. "Girl gracefully gets out of pool, soaking wet. She wants me."
2. "Beautiful stranger shows up at my door. She definitely wants
    me."
3. "Threesome. Both girls want me."
4. "Sorority house pillow fight. All the sisters want me."

The Problem with Porn

Breaking into the industry

Even your wildest fantasies sometimes fail you. You've re-created that special night one too many times. You can't see clearly. You're in need of some serious visual stimuli. Wham chicka wham wham! Enter porno.

Now we know what you're going to say: not for me. As a Catholic girl—even a modern Catholic girl—you think

It Comes Up as Movie

Trafficking in the wilds of porn can incite even the most Catholic of couples. Check out this account from one young pair:

"Brian and I were dating a few months when we decided to go away for the weekend—our first big relationship step. It all seemed very mature to this 23-year-old. He planned a romantic day exploring the scenic Connecticut River Valley. I was in love. That night, we got tipsy at the hotel bar. By the time we made it back to our room, we were both feeling pretty amorous.

"I went to the bathroom to slip into the surprise negligee I had brought. I returned to find sweet, sensitive Brian flipping through the 'first five minutes are free' porn preview channels. Shocked, I blushed and giggled. I thought I could get his mind off it by telling him that it wasn't going to happen because the room was on *my* credit card. I wasn't going to be responsible for a bill itemized with *A Tale of Two Titties*, let alone watch the smut. His response? 'I assure you, sweetie, it comes up as Movie on the bill.

porn is silly and too sleazy to take seriously. Regular sex is hard enough to get through straight-faced, so how are you supposed to use this shady variation as a bedroom aid?

It's not like you haven't noticed the adult section of your local video store. You've been curious about the pervs who pull back the red-beaded curtain and enter. You can't believe anyone confidently struts up to the counter with *Screw the Right Thing* in her hands. We understand. You are never going to spend $3.50 to actually rent that sucker in front of people.

Total anonymity.' He spoke with some authority. Some authority, I might add, that disturbed me.

"I began to flip through the channels myself and admittedly became aroused. Brian insisted it would all be in good, clean fun. I ultimately caved. We settled on the Farmer's Daughter–themed channel, and Brian hit 'select' on our remote. Nothing. He checked the batteries. Nothing. He tried another channel. Nothing. Well, he was nothing if not persistent. Brian got on the horn to the front desk and actually spoke the following words: 'Sir, I am having some problems receiving the adult entertainment. Of course I've hit "select." No, I don't want to switch rooms. Oh, I see, the red button. OK, I'll let you know if it doesn't work. . . . There we go.'

"I admit it, I got sucked in and couldn't stop watching. Brian tried to shut it off just so he could get my attention. I turned it right back on. Porn-loving Brian had converted me, but much to his dismay, I was more interested in watching the action than doing it with him.

"The next morning, we headed to the reception desk to review our bill. Still frustrated, Brian conveniently went to get the car. The desk clerk handed me the charges, saying, 'Ah, Movie. That's my favorite, too.' "

So what's a frisky Catholic girl in need of some serious fantastical help to do? Simple: cable, public-access television and more cable. That's right, late-night TV affords the viewer a feast of sensual delights—its nickname isn't Skinemax for nothing. Admit it, you've caught a glimpse here or there. When you were totally alone. And not just for a laugh. It might even have gotten you thinking.

When you finally decide to turn on the telly, your vibrator and yourself, keep in mind that like so many other naughty explorations, your first time may be more easily accomplished after a bottle of wine. (Not that we favor wildly intoxicated sexual behavior, but the only person who is going to take advantage of you here is *you*.)

Once you've lain back and taken in the sensual sights and sounds of the limber lovers on screen, you may feel you've seen the light. In that moment, you'll believe they are sexy beasts and that it's OK to be glued to the tube. Understand this: After you are totally satisfied and spent with exhaustion, you will feel more than just the usual guilt for ever having watched that filthy, filthy flick. You will, in short, feel like a complete dirtbird. On another night, however—after a few more drinks—you're likely to experiment again. Be prepared for this cycle.

The bottom line: If it works for you, go for it. But be warned that continuous porn viewing, especially on the public-access stations, is one step away from drunk-dialing 1–900 numbers. (Talk about panic. Just when you get over the immediate regret of the phone call and start feeling respectable again, you'll be slammed with a credit-card charge that's higher than heaven and into a tailspin of shame like you've never known.)

Pious Porn

Given the Church's penchant for sexual repression, it comes as no surprise that adult films, famous for their clever plays-on-words, have exploited and capitalized on Catholic jargon. Check out the titles of these naughty flicks:

Adam and Eve's House Party
Altar of Lust
Bobby Sox
Converted to Tickling
Dirty Mary
Erotic Rituals of the Latex Nun Society
Get Me to the Church on Time
Goddaughter (1–5)
Godmother (1–3)
Holy Bondage
Knocking at Heaven's Back Door
Mary! Mary!
Oh My God . . . Oh My God
Once Upon a Madonna
Praying for Passion
Saints and Sinners
Schoolgirls' Confessions

And the ultimate import:

Interno di un Convento (a.k.a *Behind Convent Walls, Within a Cloister* and *Sex Life in a Convent*)

Bible Pop Quiz

Sarah bore her last child at what age?
a.   78
b.   13
c.   21
d.   90

Answer: d (Talk about miracles!)

The Catholic Schoolgirl's Uniform
The boys react

Perhaps nothing fuels men's fantasies more than a little plaid skirt and a crisp white blouse. Just what is it about the Catholic schoolgirl's uniform? We made some calls to find out, and our guys had plenty to say. We suspect that many a late-night frolic occurred as a direct result of our interviews.

Alex, a 31-year-old Wall Street executive, normally cool and confident, melted as he blurted out that the image of a Catholic girl in uniform "is wonderful, just wonderful—the skirt is so nice and high." He explained: "I love the kilts because they are a complete and utter paradox. They're supposed to be innocent, but there is nothing innocent about it. They are simply yummy." Most men concur, raving about the irony of a good girl in a short skirt.

Some called the uniform a shield of sorts and suggested that the girl inside was (literally) trying to bust free. "It's as though the sweater is always two sizes too small," claimed Jonathan, a musician. "Maybe her mom bought her a new uniform in June, and it fit just fine. But by the time September rolled around, the girl grew breasts. Being with a babe in this plaid armor only furthered the mystique, because you did two spectacular things: You got sex, *and* you broke through a wall to get there. Once accomplished, your natural instinct was to see if it was humanly possible to do it again."

When we asked, "What about the uniform does it for you?" William, a graphic designer, responded: "It's so hot [loud groan]. They definitely don't wear any panties." We cleared up this misstatement by making him aware that not only do Catholic schoolgirls wear panties but they usually also have shorts or spandex on over their skivvies. To which he replied: "Um. That's not true. It can't be true." Then he hung up the phone.

James, a young movie producer, said: "The space in between the knee socks and the skirt. Definitely."

"You can really get to the goods quickly," mused Douglas, an MBA candidate.

"It's like this," declared David, an anesthesiologist. "No matter how bad the girl's reputation, no matter how much of a slut she might be, somebody somewhere thinks she's good enough to be in that uniform. And that's enough of a reason to try your hardest to get her out of it!"

One thing all the boys seemed to agree on is this sad fact: The response you elicit in uniform cannot be re-created once you reach the age of 19. As we were told time and time again, the uniform's sexiness is based precisely on the fact that the girl wearing it has no idea how sexy she is. By 19 (20 for a latecomer), she's wised up.

WordPlay

ADIDAS

1. German sneaker favored by soccer players and Run DMC.

2. Childhood acronym for All Day I Dream About Sex.

Case in point: Remember back to your own school days. You likely felt stupid and awkward in your uniform, not at all aware of its effect on boys. As an adult, you can dig up that plaid kilt and scratchy sweater and try to resurrect the costume of your youth. You may be in for some fun and games in the sack, but it *will never be the same*. Sadly, we must face this fact, but surprise, surprise, men don't seem to mind the effort one bit. As one friend instructed, "It's a little like sex: Even when it's bad, it's good."

Top Uniform Tricks to Get Your Guy's Attention

Rolling up your skirt is old news. So what's a schoolgirl to do to get her guy's attention? Follow these helpful hints, and he'll be singing your praises. (For the out-of-uniform set: Adapt these tips to your own look. You're sure to be a hit at any age.)

1. Show up wearing the uniform. Trust us, it's probably enough.
2. Lose the top two buttons on the Peter Pan–collared blouse.
3. After the dismissal bell, shed the boxers under your kilt.
4. Retire the standard bucks and get your tootsies into work boots (gender-bending made super-sexy). And, uh, lose the mismatched tube socks.
5. Kill the spandex and opt for silk stockings. (Thigh-highs work best.)
6. Forget your bra.
7. Put your hair up in pigtails (for the innocent look).

Hidden Assets

Stephanie leaves the house in proper uniform, but by 3 p.m. she's ready for her *Maxim* photo shoot. Demerits be damned, and with a quick sleight of hand, she goes from saintly to sexy just in time for her early afternoon date with Paul.

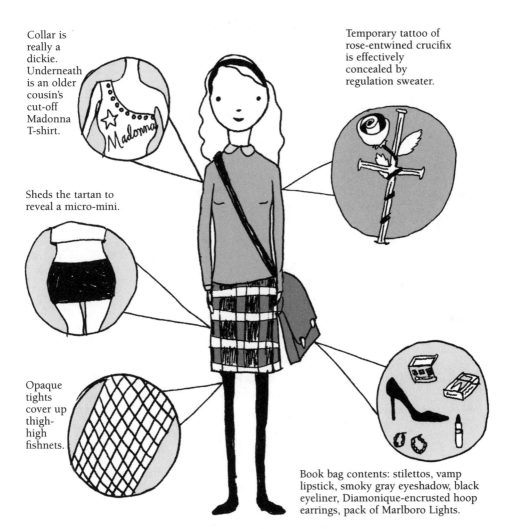

Collar is really a dickie. Underneath is an older cousin's cut-off Madonna T-shirt.

Temporary tattoo of rose-entwined crucifix is effectively concealed by regulation sweater.

Sheds the tartan to reveal a micro-mini.

Opaque tights cover up thigh-high fishnets.

Book bag contents: stilettos, vamp lipstick, smoky gray eyeshadow, black eyeliner, Diamonique-encrusted hoop earrings, pack of Marlboro Lights.

"I have this theory that, in five or six years, the virgin will come back like a bomb."

—Barbara Cartland

The Virgin Subculture

When the Big Night happens much later than you expect

You might assume that all modern Catholic girls are just like you: stuck in denial but still doing it. What you may not be

Don't Judge a Girl by Her Cover

We learned a lot from Katie. She let us into the virgin underworld. Here's her story:

"I made new friends after I graduated from college. In fact, I made a group of really good girlfriends. After a few months, we realized that our little book club was not the common bond that drew us together. One night over several—and I mean several—glasses of chardonnay, we had The Talk and found out the truth: We were all still virgins.

"It's not that all of us were clinging to our purity. We yearned for sex. Some of us just wanted it to be done in a nice enough way that we wouldn't be throwing up with guilt the next morning. A couple other girls were hoping that their Saturday-night dates would make a move. Two others in the crew seriously considered doing the nasty with the next guy who hit on them at a bar.

"We weren't just ready, we were overripe. We became obsessed. Everything in our lives began to revolve around losing our virginity. Each night, I prayed for it to happen, but I woke up every morning aware of is the considerable number of Catholic women in their twenties and beyond who have yet to experience the pleasures of the flesh. Think about it: Don't you have that one friend with whom you rarely talk sex? That particular gal who seems totally with it but that you feel sort of slutty around?

It's possible that no other group of Catholic women is as misunderstood as these never-been-laid ladies. First off, it's simply not true that all of them are saving themselves for marriage. Many would have done it already if the time and guy had ever been right. (Case in point: Iris Sullivan, 65 and unmarried.) We found virginal gals were quick to set the record straight.

with the same thought: 'Yup, still a virgin, I guess it was just a dream.'

"My fellow virgins and I met regularly—still under the auspices of book club, although I don't recall reading much. Instead, we made game plans. We critiqued outfits. We did full-on makeovers.

"Finally, one by one it started to happen for us: Jill met her perfect boy; a couple more girls persuaded their best guy friends to give them a helping hand; still others took a Club Med vacation together where anonymity and booze added up to doing the deed. All but one of us lost our virginity, and she plans to remain chaste until marriage, as originally vowed at 15. In the same way that our chats made us feel more normal about doing it, they made *her* feel more normal about not doing it. For those of us who did it, we all lost our virginity differently than we had imagined when we were teenagers. None of us cared.

"Looking perfect, flirting brilliantly and having a boyfriend all took a backseat once we had lost our collective virginity. A huge weight had been lifted and we could finally relax. This wall wasn't there anymore. In short: We realized that we were now all living in the After Sex era, or AS, and that everything prior had been Before Sex, or, plainly, BS."

"We are perceived as frigid," said Shannon. "This is definitely not true. I have desires and wants and—to be honest—some really raunchy fantasies."

Brenda agreed: "I don't need people to tiptoe around the topic. Just because I haven't done the deed doesn't mean I don't get horny. When a nonvirgin goes through a dry spell, there aren't scores of people calling her asexual. It's unfair that it happens to us."

The girls also bemoaned the fact that guys . . . well, guys just *know* if you're a virgin. And what might have been a certain medal-of-honor conquest for a high-school student or even for a college man with his young coed, becomes a veritable minefield of disaster for these same men in their twenties and thirties. On the rare occasion when

A Virgin's Prayer

"Hail, Christina the Amazing and Gertrude the Great and all the other virgin saints. Hail, Saint Rita of Cascia and Saint Gregory, patron saints of desperate cases.

"Let tonight be the night. When I come upon him tonight, let me bewilder him with romance and let him see the burning desires within me. Please let him know that I want it, too.

"Pray for me that he may be kind and handsome and ready and gentle. Pray that I might enjoy it a little.

"In the name of elder virgins everywhere, Amen."

the guy hasn't figured it out, virginity brings up a whole host of other problems. Namely, when *is* the right moment to tell your 33-year-old suitor that you have never fully rounded the bases?

When asked how much she thought Catholicism played into her late coming-of-age date, Danielle replied: "A lot. When I think about my childhood and learning about sex, faith and boys, I come to one conclusion: I was duped into believing that having sex before marriage made me a bad person. After I finally did it, I realized how dead wrong I was."

Luckily for her, Danielle got over the guilt. "Having waited so long meant I knew who I was and that sex wasn't

Never Gonna Get It, Never Gonna Get It

It's hard enough to swallow the fact that scores of holy women died virgins. More than a dozen met an even worse fate: torture and martyrdom in addition to never experiencing the pleasures of the flesh. Several were beheaded or stoned because of their refusal to become intimate with men. Saint Agatha had her breasts chopped off before being killed, Ouch. The following fourteen canonized ladies gave it (but not *It*) all away. Next time you're going through a dry spell, consider these virgin martyr saints who made the ultimate sacrifice.

Agnes (January 21)
Emerentiana (January 23)
Martina (January 30)
Agatha (February 5)
Apollonia (February 9)
Petronilla (May 31)
Maria Goretti (July 5)

Justa and Rufina (July 19)
Cecilia (November 22)
Viviana (December 2)
Leocadia (December 9)
Lucy (December 13)
Eugenia (December 25)

going to change me," she continued. "Sure, maybe this smacks in the face of my Catholic childhood, but I'm an adult now."

Eager to Please

When there is shame in being a bad lover

Just because a Catholic girl isn't ready to give it up doesn't mean she's going to leave her guy high and dry. These Catholic gals bring finesse to foreplay. Elizabeth, who remained a virgin throughout college, said:

"I became the blowjob queen of Southern California—and that's saying a lot. I had all these expectations of what men wanted: a temptress, a love slave. As a good Catholic girl, I aimed to please. I wanted to rev up my guy's drive, but I wasn't about to lose my virginity to just anyone. If I wasn't screwing him, I asked myself, how could I get him to stick around long enough to figure out if he was the one? So I gave good head. I was probably better at giving hummers than any one of my girlfriends. But I wasn't doing the deed, and somehow this made it all OK."

Catholic-girl anxiety doesn't end once you've cashed in your V-card, either. Even if you can get over the getting-it-on angst, you still might find yourself dealing with performance anxiety. Think about it: There's guilt in doing it and then there's guilt in doing it badly. We spoke to countless women who each described her sexual code in a similar manner. As Natasha put it, "I grew up trying to please everyone: my parents, my teachers, my principal, my priest. Aiming to please men came naturally."

Sure, Catholics fear the wrath of nuns in the classroom should their penmanship be out of kilter or their penance not quite contrite. But as an adult, high on the guilt list is disappointing your man. The roots took hold young, with the scary phenomenon resulting from missed attempts at pleasuring your first boyfriend. We think it all started with the dreaded "blue balls."

Love Hurts

Legends of the blue-tinged affliction made their way into gossip circles at slumber parties, in girls' bathrooms and at sports practices. For us girls raised to believe that we must always please, our mission became clear: At all costs, avoid the disastrous end result of amorous attempts gone awry.

At a certain time in your teen years, the boys around you stopped being shy about discussing the topic. Your beau might have flat-out told you that you caused him pain. But here's the secret you'll wish you knew back then. We heard this from now-enlightened men out of their teens: It's not necessarily your fault if blue balls occur. It's more likely *his* fault for getting ahead of himself. Maybe you're interested in extended foreplay, but he's ready for the main event.

So, do you add figuring out your guy's rhythm (and sacrificing your own pleasure for his) to your list of sexual anxieties? No. Bad move. You got him excited, but he got himself overexcited. You're not purposely keeping him from climax; you're just taking your time to get really hot and sexy. Get it? It's *his* job to let you know what's happening down there. Blaming you later is just pathetic.

OK, OK. To be totally honest, a real she-devil can cause pain in her man's testes. The lesson from our guys? Nobody likes a tease. It hurts the ego and it hurts down there. It also hurts a girl's rep with the boys, by the way.

Hopefully the frequency of blue balls lessens after puberty. At that point you'll probably still deal with the anxiety of being a fantastic partner. Sure, you want to be the best lover you can be and please your man better and better each time. But don't sweat it too much. As one insider told us, "It's really hard for a woman to be bad at sex. If she's willing, we're already pretty psyched."

Apologies Suck

Tara recalls her first encounter with blue balls:

"I had been dating Peter, my high-school boyfriend, for a few months. One night I was giving him a hand job. I imagined it would go further at some point, but just then I was sort of bored and not really in the mood. I was hoping to stop altogether and resume hooking up later. So I stopped, kissed him a little and just snuggled. He let out this muffled cry and seemed pissed off at me for the rest of the night.

"The next day, I discussed the situation with two of my guy friends. They were actually angry with me. They became super-animated on the subject. They sat me down and told me that I had given poor Peter blue balls. They said I owed him big time.

"Mortified at my apparent lapse in boudoir etiquette, I sucked it up and called Peter immediately to tell him I would be over for a surprise lunch. I arrived at the beach club where he lifeguarded and immediately led him to a private cabana. I feel pretty confident that the 'I'm sorry' blowjob I gave him that day is the best he's ever received."

Bible Pop Quiz

True or false: The Angel of the Lord called out, "Abraham, Abraham!" because Abraham was performing divinely.

False. (It was to spare Isaac's life.)

One of Us

From Al Capone (a killer Catholic) to Frank Zappa (um, last we checked Moon Unit and Dweezil are still not saints' names), here's a list of our favorite living and dead famous Catholics who confuse the message.

Al Capone
George Carlin
The whole Kennedy clan
Madonna
Master P
Mickey Mantle
Sean Penn
The Sex Pistols's Johnny Rotten (yup, Johnny Rotten's one of us)
Frank Sinatra
Frank Zappa

The Impurity Test

You've learned a lot. You've done a lot. You're ready for your self-evaluation. Find out if you are going to heaven or hell. Answer yes or no to the questions below and calculate your score at the end.

1. Have you ever let your mind wander at church?
2. Have you ever fantasized about sex?
3. Have you ever fantasized about sex at church?
4. Have you ever fantasized about having sex *in* church?
5. Have you ever masturbated?
6. Have you ever masturbated while talking on the phone?
7. Have you ever masturbated while talking to God?
8. Have you ever used a vibrator?
9. Have you ever used any sex toys?
10. Have you ever used a sacred relic as a sex toy?
11. Have you ever watched porn?
12. Have you ever watched porn to achieve orgasm?
13. Have you ever stayed home to watch porn while your mother believed you were at church?
14. Have you ever been on a date?
15. Have you ever been on a date that ended in a parked car at Saint Perpetua's Elementary School?
16. Have you ever kissed a boy?
17. Have you ever kissed a boy in the "crying babies room" during Mass?
18. Have you ever engaged in oral sex?
19. Have you ever engaged in oral sex on Sunday?
20. Have you ever had sexual intercourse?
21. Have you ever had sex before marriage?
22. Have you ever done it with a married person (other than your spouse)?

23. Have you tried more than five positions?
24. Have you ever tried more than five positions in one go?
25. Have you ever thanked God for giving you the strength to do more than five positions?
26. Have you ever had sexual intercourse on the first date?
27. Have you ever had sexual intercourse on a date at church?
28. Have you ever cried out the Lord's name in vain during sex?
29. Have you failed to confess to your beau the number of partners you've really had?
30. Have you failed to confess to yourself the number of partners you've really had?
31. Have you failed to confess to a priest the number of sins you've really committed?
32. Have you ever asked for sex?
33. Have you ever begged for sex?
34. Have you ever prayed for sex?

Give yourself 1 point for every yes answer, 0 for every no.

0–1: Devout Dame

You're a harlot and a liar. You can't be as pure as they come. You're going to hell.

2–16: Curious Catholic

You may indeed be a good modern Catholic girl who is inquisitive and only dabbles with the dark side, but you're still going to hell.

17–25: Member of the Cliterati

You're a member of the exclusive girls' club where finding the key to your clitoris opens the door to multiple (real) orgasms. You are going to hell.

26–34: Heathen

Nothing more to say. Start packing. You've got a ticket on the next bus to hell.

Sex Tips

Most Catholic girls are always looking for ways to better please their partners, despite denying it. Below you'll find some quick tips to spice up a dull routine. Note: Be sure to take baby steps, sister. You don't want to find yourself in too compromising a position.

1. *Morning worship.*
    Surprise him with a frolic at dawn.
2. *Sit, stand, kneel, bow your head, genuflect.*
    Plainly, if your game has gotten stale, try a new position.
3. *Oh God! Oh Derek!*
    Imagine that you're sharing a bed with your favorite short-stop. (But definitely do NOT let your guy know it.) Now pull out all the stops to ensure that he comes back for more.
4. *Find a new place of worship.*
    Make love anywhere but that same old bed. For inspiration, check out the most popular places for passion in chapter four.
5. *Put on your not-so-Sunday best.*
    In short, play dress-up. Favorite options include: cheerleader, French maid, sexy librarian and, of course, Catholic school-girl.
6. *Yes, Sister Sexy.*
    Dozens of men can't be wrong. Guys told us time and time again that the best thing a woman can do for a man in bed is simply take the initiative.

Roving Reporter

"What was your most embarrassing sexual moment?"

Vincent Kelly, 50
Married with ten kids

"My honeymoon."

Jimmy McCracken, 15
Fordham Prep sophomore

"Please, I'm the man."

Danny and Francesca Gallo, both 29
Newlyweds

Francesca answers for both:
"One time, Danny was a lil' tipsy and he couldn't . . . well, let's just say perform up to par. I got all dressed up in a go-go costume and did a little dance. But he didn't get excited. I guess he was real tired."
(In truth, Danny saw the vinyl heel of Francesca's boot and, well, shot his load right there. Francesca's go-go dance actually was performed earlier in the evening at Silk Dolls.)

Iris Sullivan, 65
Unmarried

"Confessional, 1967: I admitted my fantasies to Father Fleming. But if I knew then what I know now, I would have fulfilled them and fulfilled them some more."

Andrea Perez, 22
Recent college grad

"Oral sex. Gagged. Puked. Enough said."

Chapter Seven

The Relief

Finally: The Catholic girl's guide
to getting off (guilt-free)

> *"Sex is hardly ever just about sex."*
>
> —Shirley MacLaine

There you have it. We've revealed the modern Catholic girl's battle with big guilt. We tried to shed light on a complicated topic—the explosive mixture of Catholicism and sex. After laying the guilt on thick, we'd be remiss if we left it at that. Rest assured, we have our own stress-relief program.

In this chapter, you'll find lessons from fallen Catholics and non-Catholics alike on getting over it and getting into it so that peace can at last be with you. Welcome to the first day of your sexually liberated life. Well, almost.

> *"She had once been a Catholic, but discovering that priests were infinitely more attentive when she was in process of losing or regaining faith in Mother Church, she maintained an enchantingly wavering attitude."*
>
> —F. Scott Fitzgerald

Fallen Catholics
Rogue members of the parish

Our friend Gabriella was raised in a strict Catholic household. She attended parochial school grades 1–12. Now 30, Gabriella enjoys a very active sex life. She also harbors no bad feelings about her sexcapades. She is one of the few, the proud. She is a Catholic with no issues.

We know what you're thinking: It's impossible. Born-and-bred Catholics are inherently tormented by guilt. Not so. Or, at least, not entirely so. There is a group of Catholics who has mastered the feelings of dread in the service of making up their own rules. They're the fallen, and get this: They're not all men!

Fallen Catholic women fall into one of two camps: those who have flat-out left the Church and those who have decided upon their own moral code (one that usually spits in the face of Vatican teachings) but still consider themselves members of the congregation. Since the first group has renounced all things Catholic—we're talking Jewish converts, atheists and agnostics here—they have no need to reconcile their beliefs. They're in the happy, guilt-free land of a new faith. God bless.

The other crew of fallen women, however, intrigues and mystifies us. We wondered how they could go about doing the things they do with men at will and with whimsy, and with no remorse. We asked around. Their secret? They take what they want from the faith and leave the rest behind. Of course, we know that this makes for not-such-good Catholics in the eyes of the Church. But they don't accept that, either. They deem the mere act of believing in the basics (Jesus is the Son of God, love your neighbor, etc.) as making them worthy of God's love. And really, aren't they worthy? Aren't we all?

At first we thought the fallen girls simply weren't raised Catholic enough. But then we spoke to fallen Meredith, who did plenty of nun time and had plenty to say:

"I was raised with two very Catholic parents. We attended Mass every Sunday. I even went through a 'maybe I should be a nun' thing. I got over it by the time I was a teenager and knew I was ready for sex. Experimenting with boys just felt so good. And I figured that anything that heavenlike could only be a gift from God, so He must have intended for me to use it.

"I had the whole guilt thing going for a while, but the bottom line for me became a matter of feeling Godlike or not feeling Godlike. In the end, I felt that I was better praising Him by using the goods He gave me with no regret than by letting them wither away. And I never again felt badly about it."

Sophie added: "Look, it's like this. A lot of women have self-image problems. I even have them. We feel too fat or too ugly or too boring. But I'll be damned if I'm going to deal with those issues by day and also look at my boyfriend across a pillow after doing something that feels amazing and think I should be ashamed of myself."

We pressed on and asked how our freer friends managed a feat so monumental as turning a cheek to years of reinforced moral guilt. The answer was the same every time. It's simple: "I just don't follow the regime, and I consider myself Catholic because I just do," our friend Marianna told us. "I

WordPlay

Epiphany

1. January 6, Catholic feast day.

2. The moment a modern Catholic girl realizes that, despite what may have been preached to her, she is going to have sex as a single woman so she might as well enjoy it.

believe in Jesus, Mary and the whole bit. I think that's asking a lot of somebody. You know, to accept the miracles. I don't think the rest of it defines who I am."

That's it. That's all we got. *"Because I choose to believe what I believe."* We pushed for more, hoping there might be a how: *How* do these women come to feel so free with themselves and confident in their stance? Well, apparently there is no how for them. Like a guy asked about circumcision, you either have it or you don't. Later in this chapter, however, we outline some tips that hopefully will help get you there.

Why I Did the Deed

Fallen Catholics recall their one-night-stand rationalizations:

1. "He took a sick drum solo."
2. "I was horny."
3. "He burned me a CD and personalized the cover."
4. "His novel got a good review in the *New York Times*."
5. "His ass was rock-solid."
6. "I had nothing better to do that night."
7. "He had an accent."
8. "I figured you have to have one one-night stand in your life." (or two)
9. "He took me to a play."
10. "I had the place to myself."

Bible Pop Quiz

True or false? According to Deuteronomy 25:11–12, a woman must have her hands cut off should she touch a man's member in order to protect him from an attacker.

Answer: True

"Good girls go to heaven, bad girls go everywhere."
—Helen Gurley Brown

Our Jewish Friends React

Lessons from the get-it-on gang

WordPlay

WWJD?
What Would
Jesus Do?

We envy our fallen comrades but were left to follow their examples with no direct instructions. We needed to look beyond the Church. We were hoping to get multicultural and searched for tips from members of other religions but hit a wall early on. Mormons and Muslims have a set of sexual stigmas so severe that we look well adjusted by comparison. Hindu tips, by contrast, are illustrated explicitly in the *Kama Sutra*. Far from alleviating stress, however, the naughty poses only encourage more advanced guilty pleasures. Buddhists are on another path entirely. Protestants—at least of the WASPy kind—are notoriously private people. (Ever notice how they never seem to admit just how much gin has been drunk?)

After failing our course in world religions, we finally turned to our Jewish sisters and got the real juice. To be clear, we didn't interview any orthodox ladies but rather stuck with our reformed pals who are, as Sandra said, "louder than most women, so we'll gab it up for you."

"It's not that Jews promote premarital sex," said Sharon. "No religion does. We're just realistic. Further, we don't have a real belief in an afterlife. We're not trying to rack up any points with God." They were raised with a different outlook on sex than Catholics. There weren't a dozen laws to learn demanding celibacy. Simply put: No one ever stressed that sex could be considered a sin.

Now, don't go thinking that Jewish girls were preached promiscuity. Hardly. Most of our chums spoke of a silent introduction (like ours) to the world of sex. But the noncommunication seemed to be a general parental unease about approaching the topic with their "princesses," not the assumption of sin that shut up many Catholic parents. Jewish girls, too, had to turn to their peers. But they had a distinct advantage. Hello! Eight-week sleep-away camps are fertile grounds for sexploration.

Another reason they pass the sex stress test? In Judaism, divorce is accepted as a fact of life. Like sex, it is not a sin. Many girls grew up with recently separated parents (or aunts, uncles, family friends) who weren't ashamed of their single-again status. So the possibility of sex as an unattached adult (while maybe not totally overt) was simply a matter of fact.

Lots of our Jewish friends claimed that sex plainly made

them happier. With ecstasy levels skyrocketing, they realized that the benefits outweighed the guilt. "It's OK to do it just to improve your mood," Carrie said. "Take it from someone who didn't have sex for an entire year: It made me crazy."

Bottom line: Our Jewish friends believe we Catholic girls are crazy. "I don't know what there is to feel guilty about," Pamela said. "Sex is not going to change you, who you are or what you stand for." So, how did they come to accept their naughtier notions? Several ways.

Private "I"

Diane said: "I am never concerned about my reputation or how many people I've slept with. That's my business. I get embarrassed to admit to my girls that I slept with some loser, but I'm not bashful that I had the sex."

Lessons Learned

"When I was younger, I was only self-conscious because I hadn't had enough sex," Robin admitted. "I felt really inexperienced at 21. 'Two' sounded so prude. When I got a little older, I decided I was going to be promiscuous and claim my right to enjoy sex. I became the user. But it wasn't quite the empowering experience I thought it would be, because, of course, I was being used, too. And that doesn't feel so good to anyone. Still, I learned from every experience. Mistakes didn't make me a bad person."

Practice Makes Perfect

"Here's a tip," said Liza. "Have sex. It makes you get over a lot. I had hang-ups when I first started doing it, but after a couple of times, I thought: 'What's the big whoop?' A one-night stand might really help all you carnal Catholic chicks get over it a bit."

> "It was never dirty to me. After all, God gave us the equipment and the opportunity."
> —Dolly Parton

The Sexual Commandments

Jewish girls follow a different set of coitus commandments from us Catholic girls. Here's a glimpse:

Catholic
- "Thou shall have sex and thou shall deny it."
- "Thou shall try to talk to thy mom about sex. She shall leave the room."
- "Thou shall practice safe sex: Thou shall make him pull out."
- "Thou shall regret thy experience."
- "Thou shall keep thy lucky number below five."

Jewish
- "Thou shall have sex until thou are married. And then thou shall shop."
- "Thou shall try to talk to thy mom about sex. She won't shut up."
- "Thou shall practice safe sex: Thou shall go on the Pill at age 15 *and* insist he wear a condom."
- "Thou shall learn from thy experience."
- "Thou shall try to keep a better tally of thy lucky number."

"Every harlot was a virgin once."
—William Blake

Selma's Sayings

Our adopted Jewish grandmother had a lot to say.

- "There is something to be said for waiting. . . . You can weed out the jerks."

- "All that matters is that he's good-looking. Or that he's a doctor. Or a lawyer. Or at least he makes a lot of money."

- "You're worth dinner and wine. Don't forgo the dinner.

- "Sex is not love."

- "Don't love a man because you need him. Need him because you love him."

- "There are only two things in life that are forever: diamonds and herpes. Only catch the first one."

- "Don't wear underwear to bed. You've got to let it breathe."

"I consider promiscuity immoral. Not because sex is evil,
but because sex is too good and too important."

—Ayn Rand

Don't wear underwear to bed. You've got to let it breathe.

She Did

Sara, age 28

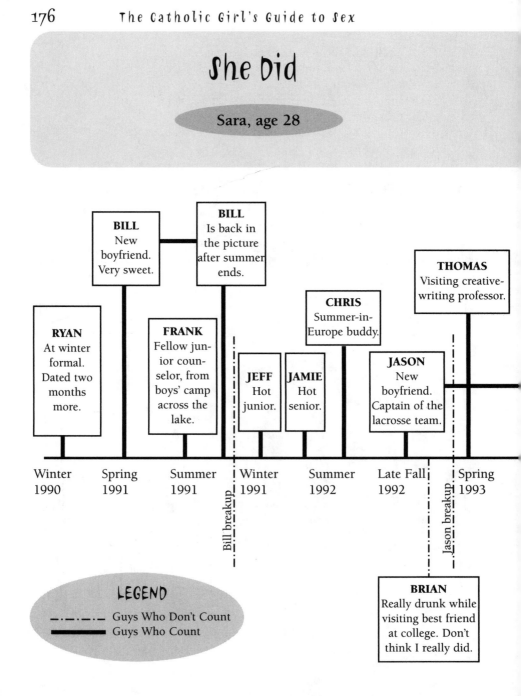

BILL
New boyfriend. Very sweet.

BILL
Is back in the picture after summer ends.

THOMAS
Visiting creative-writing professor.

RYAN
At winter formal. Dated two months more.

FRANK
Fellow junior counselor, from boys' camp across the lake.

CHRIS
Summer-in-Europe buddy.

JEFF
Hot junior.

JAMIE
Hot senior.

JASON
New boyfriend. Captain of the lacrosse team.

Winter 1990   Spring 1991   Summer 1991   Winter 1991   Summer 1992   Late Fall 1992   Spring 1993

Bill breakup

Jason breakup

BRIAN
Really drunk while visiting best friend at college. Don't think I really did.

LEGEND

–··–··– Guys Who Don't Count
—— Guys Who Count

While many Catholic girls achieve remarkable feats of concealment and acts of denial in order to maintain their idea of an acceptable reputation, thousands of other women have no such hang-ups. For a peek into the past of one such gal, check out the following graph charting Sara's sexual history. Compare it to Amanda's on page 114, and decide for yourself who's the worse for the wear.

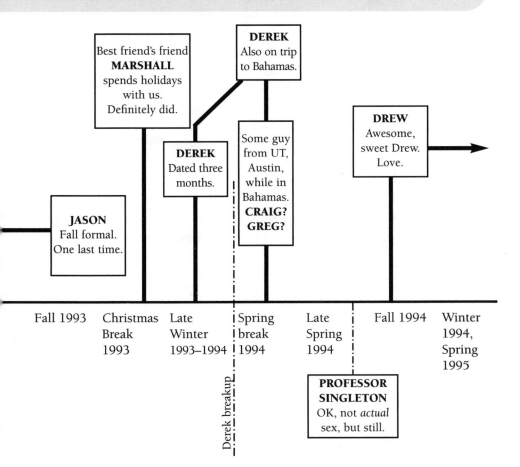

DEREK
Also on trip to Bahamas.

Best friend's friend
MARSHALL
spends holidays with us.
Definitely did.

DREW
Awesome, sweet Drew.
Love.

DEREK
Dated three months.

Some guy from UT, Austin, while in Bahamas.
CRAIG?
GREG?

JASON
Fall formal.
One last time.

| Fall 1993 | Christmas Break 1993 | Late Winter 1993–1994 | Spring break 1994 | Late Spring 1994 | Fall 1994 | Winter 1994, Spring 1995 |

Derek breakup

PROFESSOR SINGLETON
OK, not *actual* sex, but still.

Guy Guilt

Yup, that's right, it even happens to him.

You're probably thinking: impossible. Most women perceive guys as having no sexual hang-ups beyond size and stamina insecurities. We thought so, too. Truthfully, many men (Catholic and non-Catholic alike) fight emotional anxiety at least some of the time. The difference between male and female stress? For the boys, it's usually short-lived. They feel pangs of remorse but only for a moment. There is no wallowing in guy-land. After questioning several men, we have come to the conclusion that boys' bouts with guilt fall into three categories:

Samuel Monogamist

This guy can't comprehend having sex without commitment. He will only do the deed with a devoted dame; casual sex leaves him feeling too guilty. He is a rare bird. We stress *rare*.

"Sex without love is just gross," said Sam.

The Skinny: Tread with caution. It may seem sweet that he puts sex on a pedestal, but he may carry even more baggage than you. That's the last thing a Catholic girl needs. However, his relationship-status prerequisite is a good rule of thumb. You're sure to feel good in the morning after a night with a legit honey.

The Signs: He keeps the local florist on speed dial. His DVD collection includes *Love Story* and *The Story of Us*. His experienced foot-massage hands are nice, but his ring finger is definitely itching for a wedding band.

James Bondsman

Another anxious guy is the man who feels stress about love-less sex but doesn't necessarily save himself for a steady. Rather, he tries to create the illusion of a bond (a fleeting moment of intimacy) to alleviate next-day guilt.

"I think sometimes I deny the repercussions of sex," said James. "I often get caught up in courting some fine lady, only to realize that there is a void between us when we're having sex. I need to make sure she and I are on the same casual-sex page in order to commit the act. I have ways to do this. How? I am honest. I am frank about what I want for the night. If she agrees to cavort without commitment, then I'm in. I convince myself we've connected. Now I can open the guilt-free floodgates to a sex-filled evening without worrying that she'll read into my pillow talk. I am sensual. I compliment. In this way, shallow sex can seem very meaningful—in the moment, anyway. Well, at least I wake up feeling a little better."

The Skinny: Girlfriend-only-for-the-night James gets over the guilt by taking solace in the make-believe of a meaningful moment. He feigns romance only after being open and honest. You should be, too. Letting your lover know where you stand is always a good idea. But be warned, it's hard not to believe something deeper exists in the moment.

The Signs: He keeps a copy of *I'm OK—You're OK* by his bedside. He stops kissing you regularly to repeatedly ask, "You get where I'm coming from, right?"

Morning-After Phil

The guy who feels the least amount of guilt and who also does the least to prevent it is, plainly, the man your mother/father/brother warned you about. Unlike James Bondsman, this Casanova casts aside honesty and frankness about his zero-relationship potential in the service of bedding you. He'll lie, cheat and steal to win you over for one night only. Hard to believe he cares enough to feel guilty, but he does, if even only a little bit.

"I love sex," said Phil. "If I dedicated half as much time to my work as I do to getting women in the sack, I'd probably have a multibook contract, a Pulitzer and a couple of movie deals. Instead, I bartend part-time. Meanwhile, my sex life thrives.

"My secret is simple: I feign just enough interest to make a girl feel special, but also maintain enough distance to keep her wanting more. I will say almost anything in the heat of the moment to get a girl naked. I won't tell a lady I love her if it's not true, but I know plenty of dudes who will.

"You might think I'm a heartless jerk. And you're almost right, except for the fact that most mornings I get up with my conscience calling. When I wake up sober, I realize that I have used the girl lying nude beside me, and, since I gave her no indication of this, she has no idea.

"I try to make amends. I will likely take her to brunch and pay her cab fare home. These girls leave my company the same way every time: I give them a platonic kiss on the cheek and a promise of a phone call.

"By the time Sunday football is over, so are my pangs of guilt. From kickoff through the final touchdown, I have rationalized some combination of the following: 1) She was just in it for the sex, too; 2) she's psychotic; and 3) no woman (except mom) is worth the headache of feeling bad about something."

The Skinny: First, realize that no one man (not even the Pope) is worth the aggravation of feeling bad about. Second, if you're looking for something beyond a romp in the hay, never trust what a boy says in bed. If you take the time to get to know (and even love) your guy before you do the deed, you're less likely to fall into a guilt trap.

The Signs: He has a six-poster, fake sunset montage in his bedroom. You're pretty sure he hit on your friend while you made a trip to the ladies room. Forget one-handed bra maneuvers, this guy got your whole blouse off with a flip of the wrist.

Help from the Pros (and Even a Con)

Tips for alleviating your angst

If anxiety still rules your outlook, despite the lessons learned from our fallen comrades and our friends of many faiths, relax. (Seriously, relax!) This is a full-service book, and we've got it covered. We combed through advice from experts (armchair and real doctors alike) and picked out Dos and Don'ts for you, dear reader.

DO:

- Mother Teresa it. Get out there and volunteer. It's good for the guilt and the soul.
- Get shopping. Every girl knows that retail relief is seri-

ous therapy. However, charge responsibly. Don't drag yourself to the mall if:

    a. Your finances are in such bad order that you keep your credit card locked in the freezer.

    b. Trying on bathing suits might be involved.

- Book an aromatherapy massage. Tip: Don't enlist your lover to do the rubbing, since it's the stress of his moves that you are seeking to relieve.
- Shake your groove thing. From releasing energy to improving sleep, dancing helps in so many ways. Plus, your new fab body will automatically make you feel great.

DON'T:

- Forget you're not alone.
- Believe you're crazy.
- Think you're a terrible person for having sexual urges.
- Measure your own sexual guidelines against another's, especially when that other is a celibate man.

We Didn't Even Ask—He Answered Anyhow

WordPlay

Group Therapy

An orgy.

When discussing the topic of stress relief with a couple of our guy friends, they had a lot to say, succinctly. So here it is, unedited—the boys' answers to stress relief (take them with a large grain of salt):

1. If your stress is over oral sex, try performing it first thing in the morning, so you have the whole day to put it out of your mind.

2. If your stress is over having sex, have lots more sex. It works.
3. If your stress is leading to sleepless nights, have sex as a way to relax. If you're anything like us, you'll be snoring seconds after finishing.
4. If your stress is manifested during office hours, have a quickie under your desk.
5. If your stress is over kinky sex, please call us. Today.

"Catholicism is not a soothing religion. It's a painful religion. We're all gluttons for punishment."

—Madonna

Truth in Packaging: Shame Versus Guilt

There is a distinction between guilt and shame. Throughout this book, for the most part we have talked about feeling guilty—something most of us normally feel at different times in our lives. It's something a good laugh can help undo. Shame, though, can be far more serious and destructive.

Guilt is healthy when kept in check. It guides our moral choices (a little guilt goes a long way.) Guilt is feeling bad about something you've done or haven't done. Shame, however, is feeling bad about *yourself*. The next time pious panic sets in, try to figure out which emotion you're feeling. If you feel shame late one night, you might consider a therapist to help you work through your issues. There is definitely no shame in that.

If what you feel is guilt, you're in luck, because it should go away once you've apologized and made amends. Know this: Forgiveness is always available in the Catholic Church. Jesus hung out with tax collectors, prostitutes and a legion of sinners. Why? Because God is loving and forgiving. Once excused, that's it: You're excused. No guilt allowed. Remember, it doesn't matter what someone judgmental thinks; it only matters what He thinks. Heavy stuff, but whoo-hoo for us!

Bible Pop Quiz

What did Jacob do almost as soon as he met Rachel?
a. Fondled her ta-tas.
b. Asked for her hand.
c. Kissed her.
d. "Cheered" her up.

Answer: c

The Parental Years

All grown up

We like to believe that one day we modern Catholic girls will successfully toe the line between raising our daughters with a strong sense of faith and bringing them up to be well-adjusted young adults. Doubtful, but we can hope. To that end, we vow to do certain things along the way.

A Pledge for Future Catholic Mothers

"I, _____, vow to do the very best to raise my daughter as a good Catholic but also a smart one. I will foster an environment of unconditional love and acceptance. I will talk with her about sex at an early enough age that she won't be misinformed by playground Johnny-come-stupids. I will instill in her a sense of respect. I vow to educate her in the ways of men and remind her that she should not have sex with a man (or a woman), lest she desire to remember his (or her) name for the rest of her life. Birth control will be an open discussion. I vow to avoid the topic of masturbation, except to tell her it's natural (and not a sin in my eyes) but leave the rest to self-exploration. I will let her know that whatever the issue, she should come to her mother first. I vow to use guilt as a manipulation tool only when it comes to hard work, discipline, visiting Grandma and really, really slutty behavior."

"Sex is like money; only too much is enough."
—John Updike

Roving Reporter

"How do you know you're really a Catholic?"

Vincent Kelly, 50
Married with ten kids

> "Because every time I see a Trojan ad, I say a Novena, praying that the Vatican will change its rules before my youngest ones get to college."

Jimmy McCracken, 15
Fordham Prep sophomore

> "Because my mom wakes me up every Sunday morning for stupid church."

Danny and Francesca Gallo, both 29
Newlyweds

Francesca answers for both:
"Because we could never have conceived of getting married anywhere else but our local chapel."
(In truth, the *real* wedding took place two months prior at Elvis's Chapel of Love in Las Vegas. Though Danny attends Mass weekly, Francesca hasn't been inside a church since her Confirmation. The only "conceiving" that took place occurred in their room at the Flamingo.)

Iris Sullivan, 65
Unmarried

> "Years of reinforced guilt. But if I knew then what I know now, I'd have converted and converted some more."

Andrea Perez, 22
Recent college grad

> "Because I still feel guilty whenever my mom calls to ask me to phone Aunt Ethel, see if I got ashes, find out what I did last night, comment on my eating habits, etc."

Are You Just Too Catholic for Sex?

You've been with us on our journey from devout to devilish. The question remains: Where in the sexual spectrum do you lie? Take this quiz to find out whether there's a sexual revolution in your future:

1. After reading this book, you felt:
    a. Relieved to know there are others just like you.
    b. A little horny.
    c. That the two authors should be ashamed of themselves and clearly are going straight to hell.

2. The section you most related to was:
    a. Communication, because if you'd gotten pregnant every time a guy told you a birth-control lie, you'd be the mother of at least nine by now.
    b. Anything and everything about masturbation.
    c. The parts that reiterate the Church's view.

3. If you were to attend Catholic school today, you would probably embellish your uniform a bit with the help of:
    a. Knee-high black leather boots.
    b. A red-lace push-up bra and V-neck T-shirt.
    c. Scissors to let *down* the too-high hem.

4. When you think about your next sexual experience, you mostly think about:
    a. Your sexy boyfriend.
    b. Your sexy boyfriend and his hot roommate.
    c. The confessional.

5. If you were advising a teenage girl about sex, you would mostly likely:
    a. Go through the basics and honestly answer her embarrassing questions.
    b. Tell her about the new birth-control patch and how to spot a real loser boyfriend.
    c. Tell her to wash out her mouth with soap and holy water immediately.

Now, tally up your answers. Learn your score, and more, below:

Mostly as:

You're a girl who knows what you want and enjoy it when you get it. Sure, you deal with guilt, but you're learning how to maintain a healthy self-image. You are a modern Catholic girl.

Mostly bs:

You have likely left the faith. You are so OK with doing it that your next book purchase will likely be a guide to wild, kinky sex. You're ready for anything. You are definitely a non-Catholic modern girl.

Mostly cs:

You hold true the Vatican's preachings as ultimate guidance. Clearly sex is a highly controversial topic for you. If this works, go for it. You're probably more of a mom's-generation modern Catholic girl. Don't fret. There are plenty of dad's-generation modern Catholic boys out there waiting to meet you. We think.

Beyond the Bible

Here's a hit list of books, movies and websites for the modern Catholic girl. From learning more to doing more, these recommendations include Church teachings, sex tips, sources and even just good stuff we love.

Church Teachings

Books

Catechism of the Catholic Church (Doubleday, 1995). The Vatican's official word.

O'Conner, John. *The Essential Catholic Handbook.* (Liguori Publications, 1997. The middle ground between the other two.

O'Gorman, Robert T., *The Complete Idiot's Guide to Understanding Catholicism.* (Alpha Books, 2000). The name speaks for itself.

Websites

www.catholic.net—Catholic Information Center.

www.nccbuscc.org/movies—Must-read movie reviews from the U.S. Conference of Catholic Bishops.

www.trainupachild.com—Educational toys you've got to see to believe.

www.vatican.va—Official Vatican website.

For Better Sex

Books

Comfort, Alex. *The New Joy of Sex: A Gourmet Guide to Lovemaking in the Nineties*. Pocket Books, 1992. Illustrated help on all things sex.

Dodson, Betty. *Sex for One: The Joy of Selfloving*. Harmony, 1987. The masturbation manual.

Hooper, Anne J. *Anne Hooper's Kama Sutra*. DK Publishing, 1994. Easy-to-follow instructions for hot nights.

Penney, Alexandra. *How to Make Love to a Man*. Clarkson Potter, 1988. Guide to satisfying your lover's needs.

Queen, Carol. *Exhibitionism for the Shy: Show Off, Dress Up and Talk Hot*. Down There Press, 1995. Shedding your inhibitions.

Westheimer, Dr. Ruth K. *Sex for Dummies*. Hungry Minds, 2000. The ultimate sexpert shares her wisdom in the "Dummies" format.

Winks, Cathy. *The Good Vibrations Guide: The G-Spot*. Down There Press, 1998. A road map to your pleasure place.

Websites

www.churchsluts.com—Isn't the name enough of an invite?

www.divine-interventions.com—Sex toys for fallen Catholics only.

www.goaskalice.columbia.edu—Sex Q&A.

www.nerve.com—Intellectual smut.

www.plannedparenthood.org—The official site.

www.salon.com/sex—Literati sex.

www.singlecatholics.com—Find your mate online.

Shops
Condomania
800.926.6366/www.condomania.com
Eve's Garden
800.848.3837/www.evesgarden.com
Good Vibrations
800.289.8423/www.goodvibes.com
My Pleasure
866.697.5327/ww.mypleasure.com
Sinclair Intimacy Institute
800.955.0888/www.bettersex.com
Toys in Babeland
800.658.9119/www.babeland.com
Xandria
800.242.2823/www.xandria.com

For Kicks and Giggles

Books
Blume, Judy. *Are You There God? It's Me, Margaret.* Bradbury Press, 1970. Elementary-school required reading for girls who want to be in-the-know.
Bushnell, Candace. *Sex and the City.* Warner Books, 1997. The real Carrie Bradshaw in her own words.
Cavolina, Mary Jane Frances, et al. *Growing Up Catholic: The Commemorative Catholic Jubilee Edition.* Broadway Books, 2000. Explores what's funny about being Catholic.
Cawthorne, Nigel. *Sex Lives of the Popes.* Prion, 1997. Find out how some Church leaders put us to shame.
Fielding, Helen. *Bridget Jones's Diary.* Viking, 1998. Must-read for the twenty- and thirtysomething set, for laughter therapy.
Karp, Marcella, and Debbie Stoller, eds. *The Bust Guide to the New Girl Order.* Penguin Press, 1999. Witty, first-person essays on all things woman.

Big Screen/On Stage

The Brothers McMullen, (directed by Ed Burns). 1995. Irish brothers drink and talk love.

Everything You've Always Wanted to Know About Sex but Were Afraid to Ask (directed by Woody Allen). 1972. The title says it all.

Godfather trilogy (directed by Francis Ford Coppola). 1992. Unholier than thou Italian-American saga.

Heaven Help Us (directed by Michael Dinner). 1985. Parochial-school pranksters.

The Kentucky Fried Movie (directed by John Landis). 1977. Your boyfriend will appreciate this one.

Late Nite Catechism, by Maripat Donovan and Vicki Quade. Years of CCD in one comedic night.

Monty Python's The Meaning of Life (directed by Terry Gilliam and Terry Jones). 1983. Large Irish families explained.

Sister Mary Ignatius Explains It All for You, by Christopher Durang. Listen up.

Superstar (directed by Bruce McCulloch). 1999. Mary Catherine Gallagher takes the cool out of schoolgirl.

About the Authors

Melinda Anderson and Kathleen Murray live in New York City. They pray for forgiveness.